1963

WHAT A YEAR TO BE BORN!

Written by
Robin Bennett-Freebairn and Joe Toussaint

Published by Emersive
🌐 whatayeartobeborn.com

What happened in 1963? We all have a special affinity for the year we were born, but how much do we really know about it? This guide takes you through the highs and lows of an historic year towards the end of the baby boom generation. The colour-coded chapters hold a wealth of information that bring you closer to what life was like in this milestone year.

Contents

▶ Introduction

On New Year's Day, Great Britain woke up still in the grip of a big freeze. The harsh weather would persist until 6th March. Those born in 1963 were among the very last to be part of the post-war population bulge which defined those born between 1946 and 1964 as "Baby Boomers". The most popular girls' names of the year were Susan, Julie and Karen, for boys it was David, Paul and Andrew. The year was a momentous and tumultuous one both in Britain and across the world. At home "Beatlemania" was born. The Fab Four played concert after concert to screaming fans, enjoying hit after hit that included three number 1s. It wasn't only in music that there was a seismic shift away from the more austere decade of the 1950s; the fashions of the day were also changing. Women were keen to sport a bikini on the beach and Capri pants, cropped slim trousers, when out on the town. Many men in the early '60s embraced "Mod" fashion, which ironically, far from looking forward, embraced the style of the Edwardian era, including three piece suits, cravats and crisp-pointed collared shirts.

At a time when the young of the country were embracing change, drinking in coffee shops, frequenting music clubs and, if they could afford it, riding mopeds, the political elite seemed out of step. Prime Minister Harold Macmillan had served with distinction in the First World War, but that seemed a distant memory to the youth of '63. All too soon the Conservative Government would be mired in scandal. The Secretary of State for War, John Profumo, had embarked on an ill-advised affair with a 19-year-old model, Christine Keeler. She was also in a relationship with a Russian naval attaché. Profumo resigned after lying to parliament with the "affair" playing a large part in the fall of the Macmillan administration. After the prime ministers resignation the Tories appointed Alec Douglas-Home as leader and PM, who if anything he seemed more aloof than his predecessor. Meanwhile Harold Wilson, who replaced Hugh Gaitskell as Labour leader after his untimely death, could paint himself as a man of the people.

On 8th August news broke of what was to be dubbed "The Great Train Robbery", where a team of fifteen armed robbers made off with over 2 million pounds. In sport, Henry Cooper ever so nearly beat Cassius Clay in a fight filled with controversy. Tottenham Hotspur became the first British club to lift a European trophy. In rugby, the Welsh minnows of Newport beat the mighty All Blacks. In film, Cliff Richard was off on his *Summer Holiday*, whilst many became wary of crows after watching Hitchcock's *The Birds*. The world also lost two of its greatest poets, Robert Frost and Sylvia Plath.

It was a year of great speeches from Martin Luther King's "I Have a Dream," to JFK's "Ich bin ein Berliner" and to Haile Selassie's "All Around is War." On 22nd November all other events of the year paled into insignificance when it was announced that President John F. Kennedy had been assassinated.

The Daily Headlines

No: 5496

THREE PENCE

First Edition

Thursday, August 8, 1963

THE GREAT TRAIN ROBBERS STEAL OVER £2 MILLION IN AUDACIOUS AND BRUTAL ATTACK

The Daily Headlines

THREE PENCE

Wednesday, August 28, 1963

No: 5516

First Edition

DR. MARTIN LUTHER KING JR. DELIVERS "I HAVE A DREAM" SPEECH IN WASHINGTON, D.C.

The Daily Headlines

THREE PENCE

Friday, October 18, 1963

No: 5563

First Edition

DOGGED BY SCANDAL AND HEALTH SCARES PRIME MINISTER HAROLD MACMILLAN RESIGNS

The Daily Headlines

No: 5565

THREE PENCE

First Edition

Friday, November 22, 1963

GLOBAL SHOCK AS PRESIDENT JOHN F. KENNEDY IS ASSASSINATED IN DALLAS, TEXAS

Jan 1ˢᵗ   Britain welcomes the New Year in. It is covered in snow and ice, much as it has been for most of the last month.

Jan 7ᵗʰ   Granada Television first broadcasts *World in Action*, a current affairs programme. Its first episode concerns itself with the atomic arms race.

Jan 11ᵗʰ   Cliff and friends are first seen heading off on their summer holidays to Europe aboard an iconic red London bus, in the film *Summer Holiday*. I guess they will be going for a week or two.

Jan 14ᵗʰ   Following his election as Governor of Alabama, George Wallace delivers a speech in which he proclaims "segregation now, segregation tomorrow, segregation forever".

Jan 14ᵗʰ   After a distinguished military career, an up-and-coming politician by the name of Jimmy Carter is elected to the Georgia State Senate.

Jan 18ᵗʰ   The opposition Labour leader, Hugh Gaitskell, dies suddenly.

Jan 23ʳᵈ   Double agent Kim Philby disappears from Beirut, Lebanon. He is bound for Moscow to seek refuge with his paymasters.

Jan 29ᵗʰ   French President Charles De Gaulle says "Non, non, non!" as he vetoes the United Kingdom's entry into the European Economic Community.

Feb 6ᵗʰ   Her Majesty Queen Elizabeth II arrives in New Zealand on the Royal Yacht *Britannia*.

Feb 11ᵗʰ   The Beatles record their debut album, *Please Please Me*, in a single day at Abbey Road Studios in London's St John's Wood. There is a rather inviting zebra crossing outside of the studio.

Feb 14ᵗʰ   The Labour Party elects 46-year-old Huyton MP Harold Wilson as its new leader. Missing out in the leadership contest is Cardiff South East MP James Callaghan. Opinion polls are currently showing strong support for the Labour Party, with a general election due before the end of next year.

Feb 16ᵗʰ   German-American philosopher Hannah Arendt coins the term "The

Banality of Evil" when describing Nazi Adolph Eichmann in her paper, *Eichmann in Jerusalem: A Report on the Banality of Evil.*

Mar 4th   In France, six people are sentenced to death for conspiring to assassinate President Charles De Gaulle. Five of the conspirators are pardoned by De Gaulle, the sixth is executed by firing squad.

Mar 5th   In Camden, Tennessee, country music star Patsy Cline (Virginia Patterson Hensley) is killed in a plane crash along with fellow performers Hawshaw Hawkins and Cowboy Copas. They were returning from a benefit gig for recently deceased DJ "Cactus" Jack Call's widow.

Mar 5th   At the Golden Globes, it's a good day for the Brits. *Lawrence of Arabia* wins best film, its director David Lean wins Best Director and Angela Lansbury wins the Best Supporting Actress Award for her role in *The Manchurian Candidate*. Rita Tushingham and Peter O'Toole are noted as Most Promising Newcomers.

Mar 6th   The Big Freeze becomes the Big Melt. The long winter of 1962/63 finally comes to an end. Temperatures rise to 17°C (62.6°F) and the remaining snow and ice disappear. The thaw is gradual, and unlike in the winter of 1947 there is no widespread flooding.

Mar 15th   In a landmark case in the law of Judicial Review it is decided that Brighton's police chief Charles Ridge has been unfairly dismissed. The case Ridge v. Baldwin marked a watershed in the British criminal justice system, placing natural justice above administrative decisions.

Mar 16th   England beat Scotland 10-8 to win the Calcutta Cup and win Rugby Union's Five Nations tournament. Wales finish last and collect the "Wooden Spoon".

Mar 21st   The Alcatraz Federal Penitentiary on Alcatraz Island in San Francisco Bay closes. The last 27 prisoners are transferred to other establishments on the order of Attorney General, Robert F. Kennedy. The prisoners included Robert Stroud, the Birdman of Alcatraz.

Mar 23rd   The 109th Boat Race takes place on the River Thames. It sees the Dark Blues

of Oxford triumph over the Light Blues of Cambridge by five boat-lengths. The race is umpired by Gerald Ellison, the Bishop of Durham, who had rowed for Oxford in the early thirties.

Mar 25ᵗʰ   London born Terence O'Neill succeeds Viscount Brookeborough as Prime Minister of Northern Ireland. He brings a forward-looking outlook to the Province, with the ambition to end sectarianism and an aspiration to revive Northern Ireland's industrial sector.

Mar 27ᵗʰ   The Chairman of British Railways, Dr. Richard Beeching, issues a report calling for sweeping cuts to the rail network. This is expected to result in the closure of more than 2,000 railway stations as well as the loss of up to 68,000 jobs and the scrapping of some 8,000 carriages.

Mar 30ᵗʰ   The 117ᵗʰ running of the Grand National Steeplechase at Aintree goes to 66-1 outsider Ayala, ridden by Pat Buckley and trained by Keith Piggott, Lester's father.

Apr 4ᵗʰ   The airline British Overseas Airways Corporation (BOAC) launches New Zealand's first jet-powered air service between Auckland Whenuapai and London Heathrow using the de Havilland Comet. The journey takes over 37 hours with stops in Sydney, Darwin, Singapore, Rangoon, Karachi, Beirut and Rome.

Apr 5ᵗʰ   The Soviet Union accepts an American proposal to establish a Moscow-Washington hotline so that the leaders of the two nations can communicate directly with each other in order to avoid war.

Apr 8ᵗʰ   The 35ᵗʰ Academy Awards ceremony is held at The Santa Monica Civic auditorium in California. It is hosted by Frank Sinatra. Best Picture and Best Director go to David Lean's *Lawrence of Arabia*. Gregory Peck and Anne Bancroft scoop Best Actor and Best Actress Awards for *To Kill a Mockingbird* and *The Miracle Worker* respectively. Thomas John Howells becomes the first Welsh Oscar winner with his documentary *Dylan Thomas*.

Apr 9ᵗʰ   Winston Churchill is granted honorary citizenship of the United States. It was the birthplace of his mother Jennie Spencer-Churchill, née Jerome.

Apr 15th Seventy thousand marchers arrive in London. They have marched from the Government's Atomic Weapons Establishment in Aldermaston, Berkshire. A separate group, "Spies for Peace", set up a picket at a nuclear bunker in Reading.

Apr 20th After fifteen years of access, the caves at Lascaux are closed to the general public in order to protect the cave paintings which are more than 17,000 years old. The paintings had been rediscovered on the 12th September 1940 in the caverns in south-western France. After opening in 1948, the paintings began to erode from carbonic acid produced by the breath of visitors.

Apr 27th American Bob Hayes becomes the first athlete to break the 10 second barrier in the 100m sprint. However, his record is not recognised as the wind was faster than 5 metres per second in his favour.

May 1st 88-year-old Sir Winston Churchill announces his retirement. He will stay on as an MP until Parliament's dissolution, but will not seek re-election.

May 1st American mountaineer Jim Whittaker and Sherpa guide Nawang Gombu become the fifth and sixth people to reach the summit of Mount Everest. In doing so, Whittaker becomes the first American to achieve the feat.

May 5th After 18 years of denial, the Soviet Union confirms that they had found and identified the remains of Adolph Hitler on the 30th April 1945.

May 8th The body of graduate student Beverly Samans is discovered. She is the tenth victim of Alberto DaSalvo, the Boston Strangler.

May 10th After weeks of unrest a settlement is reached between the Southern Christian Leadership Conference (SCLC) and the leading business owners of Birmingham Alabama. The SCLC agree to call off its boycott of local retailers, who in return "agreed to desegregate lunch counters, rest rooms, fitting rooms and drinking fountains" and to hire more African-Americans for sales and clerical jobs.

May 14th The Rolling Stones sign their first recording contract after talent scout Dick Rowe asks them to audition for Decca Records.

May 15ᵗʰ   Housewife Jean Nidetch founds Weight Watchers. The first meeting is held in a loft above a cinema in Little Neck in the New York borough of Queens.

May 17ᵗʰ   The Front de Libération du Québec, a Canadian Marxist-Leninist separatist movement, plants 11 bombs in the town of Westmount. They are timed to explode in the middle of the night. Most are successfully defused but one critically wounds military bomb disposal expert Walter Leja. He survives and is awarded the George Medal.

May 25ᵗʰ   The Organisation of African Unity (OAU) is established in Addis Ababa, Ethiopia, by representatives of 32 African nations.

May 25ᵗʰ   In a tournament much disrupted by the harsh winter of 1962/3, a crowd of nearly 100,000 watches Manchester United defeat Leicester City 3-1 in the F.A. Cup Final. Denis Law is among the scorers for United.

May 27ᵗʰ   Columbia Records release *The Freewheelin' Bob Dylan*, the artist's second studio album. It opens with the track *Blowin' in the Wind*.

May 30ᵗʰ   Coca-Cola launch its first diet drink "TaB Cola." It has only one calorie per six-ounce serving. Sugar has been replaced by saccharin.

Jun 2ⁿᵈ   Benjamin Britten's *A Hymn of St. Columba* premieres at Gartan in County Donegal, Ireland.

Jun 3ʳᵈ   It is announced that Pope John XXIII has died aged 81. His time of death is given as 7.49am and it leaves the papacy 'sede vacante'.

Jun 5ᵗʰ   British Secretary of State for War, John Profumo, resigns after revelations of an affair between him and Christine Keeler and Profumo's subsequent admission that he had lied about the affair to his fellow MPs in Parliament.

Jun 6ᵗʰ   Chairman Mao of China sends a letter to Soviet Premier Khrushchev stating that "The Chinese people will never accept the privileged position of one or two superpowers with a monopoly on nuclear weapons". He then gives the go ahead for China to accelerate its own nuclear programme.

Jun 10th   Silent movie actress Anita King dies. In 1916 she became the first woman to drive a car across the United States.

Jun 11th   South Vietnamese Buddhist monk, Thích Quảng Đức, kills himself by self-immolation. He burns himself to death at a busy intersection in Saigon to protest against the government. AP photographer Malcolm Browne was among the press who were forewarned of the event, but he was the only one on the scene. His shocking photographs quickly spread around the world.

Jun 13th   At the 36th Scripps National Bee, eighth-grader Glen Van Slyke III of Oak Ridge, Tennessee, wins the competition by correctly spelling the final word "equipage". It means a horse-drawn carriage with attendants.

Jun 16th   Russain Valentina Vladimirovna Tereshkova becomes the first woman in space on-board Vostok 6. She orbits the Earth 48 times and spends 3 days in space.

Jun 21st   White smoke is seen emanating from the chimney at the Vatican to signify that a new Pope has been chosen. He is Giovanni Battista Enrico Antonio Maria Montini, who will rule as Pope Paul VI.

Jun 26th   President JFK arrives in Ireland for a four-day visit to Europe. He is greeted at Dublin Airport by President De Valera. His motorcade to Phoenix Park is met by huge crowds who line O'Connell Street and Dame Street. Then he travels to Berlin to deliver his famous "Ich bin ein Berliner" speech.

Jun 29th   The New York Journal publishes a story headlined "High U.S. Aide Implicated in V-Girl Scandal". Included in the article by James D. Horan and Dom Frasca, is a mention that a call-girl Suzy Chang, was a "former paramour" of "one of the biggest names in American politics." When Attorney General Robert F. Kennedy finds out that they are referring to his brother, President John F. Kennedy, he summons the journalists to Washington and pressures them to halt their investigations.

Jul 1st   Five digit ZIP codes are introduced nationwide in America. The U.S. Post Office Department even uses Mr. ZIP, a caricature of a mail carrier, to encourage people to include the ZIP code in all mailings.

Jul 5th The U.S. Senate sets a new record for the briefest session by meeting at 9:00 am, and then adjourning three seconds later. There are only two Senators present for the meeting. The previous record for brevity had been a five-second meeting on the 4th September 1951.

Jul 6th The Roman Catholic Church relaxes its ban on cremations. Pope Paul VI states that "the burning of the body, after all, has no effect on the soul, nor does it inhibit Almighty God from re-establishing the body."

Jul 8th The comic strip *Fred Basset* first appears in the Daily Mail. Created by Scottish cartoonist Alex Graham, it features the adventures of the eponymous basset hound.

Jul 13th Bob Charles defeats Phil Rodgers in a 36-hole play-off to win the British Open. Charles becomes the first left-handed golfer to win a major.

Jul 19th A 25lb (11 kg) bomb is inadvertently dropped on downtown San Francisco by a US Navy Reserve pilot on a routine exercise flight. The unarmed bomb falls at the intersection of Market Street and Front Street, bounces over the eight-storey tall IBM building and damages another building three blocks away. Miraculously no one is injured.

Jul 22nd *Please Please Me* becomes the first Beatles' album to be released in America.

Jul 24th President John F. Kennedy hosts a group of American high school students who are part of the Boys Nation event sponsored by the American Legion. Among the attending students is a young man by the name of Bill Clinton.

Aug 3rd The Beatles perform for the 275th and final time at the Cavern Club in their home city of Liverpool.

Aug 3rd Stephen Ward, an osteopath caught up in the Profumo scandal, takes his own life. In his suicide note he wrote "It's a wish not to let them get me. I'd rather get myself."

Aug 5th Craig Breedlove sets a new world record to become the fastest driver in the world. He reaches a top speed of over 428mph in his vehicle *Spirit of America* at Bonneville Salt Flats in Utah.

Aug 8th   A gang intercept a train between Glasgow and London. They escape with over £2 million. To date it is the largest sum ever stolen in Britain. Newspapers are quick to dub it "The Great Train Robbery".

Aug 9th   Patrick Bouvier Kennedy, two-year-old son of Jacqueline and President John F. Kennedy, dies of infant respiratory distress syndrome.

Aug 14th   Police arrest five people suspected to have been members of the gang that had carried out the robbery of the Glasgow-London mail train the previous week. However, they only recover £100,000 (out of more than £2 million) of the cash that had been stolen.

Aug 15th   Henry Burnett, aged 21, is hanged at Cairncross Prison in Aberdeen for the murder of love-rival, seaman Thomas Guyan.

Aug 20th   In the Bristol South East by-election, Tony Benn, who had been forced to give up the seat in 1961 when he was elevated to the House of Lords, regains his seat in the Commons. The Peerage Act of 1963 allowed him to renounce the title of Viscount Stansgate. Benn wins nearly 80% of the vote.

Aug 28th   Dr. Martin Luther King Jr. delivers his "I Have a Dream" speech at a civil rights march in Washington D.C.

Aug 30th   The audio cassette and cassette player are introduced to the world by the electronics giant Philips at a technology fair in Berlin.

Sep 1st   An unidentified visitor to Lenin's Mausoleum in Moscow, enters the shrine and detonates a bomb concealed under his coat, killing himself and causing an unspecified amount of damage and injuries. Rumours circulate but the event is not reported in the Soviet press.

Sep 13th   In the showbiz wedding of the year, singer and actress Barbra Streisand marries actor Elliot Gould.

Sep 16th   The science fiction programme *The Outer Limits* premieres on the ABC television network in America. Its first episode is titled *The Galaxy Being*. It is an instant hit with audiences.

Sep 16th   The Welsh newspaper *The Western Mail* launches a fundraising campaign to replace a stained glass window which was damaged in the bombing of a church in Birmingham Alabama, by the Ku Klux Klan. The £500 target is reached within a couple of days.

Sep 20th   President John F. Kennedy proposes a joint US-Soviet voyage to the moon.

Sep 25th   The Denning Report on the Profumo Affair is published in London. The report conveniently concludes that Prime Minister Harold MacMillan and his entire cabinet had not been aware of the foibles of the Secretary of State for War even though the Whip's office had earlier warned John Profumo to end the affair.

Oct 4th   The U.S. First Lady Jacqueline Kennedy arrives in Greece. Her host is shipping magnate Aristotle Onassis, who divorced his wife Tina in 1960.

Oct 5th   In front of a crowd of 101,209, the Geelong Cats defeat the Hawthorn Hawks 109-60 to win the Grand Final of the Victoria "Aussie Rules" Football League.

Oct 6th   Six weeks before President Kennedy is due to fly to Texas, the FBI remove a certain Lee Harvey Oswald from its watch list.

Oct 9th   The Vajont Dam in Italy is breached. Though the dam does not collapse the overflowing water floods the city of Longarone, killing over 2,000 people.

Oct 10th   Attorney General Robert F. Kennedy approves the wire-tapping of Martin Luther King Jr.'s home after discussions with FBI chief J. Edgar Hoover.

Oct 16th   Metaphorical white smoke emerges from the committee rooms of Parliament as Conservative Grandees appoint Alec Douglas-Home to the position of Prime Minister. There is no election.

Oct 16th   Lee Harvey Oswald gets a job at the Texas School Book depository. The rate of pay is $208.82 per month.

Oct 18th   Prime Minister Harold Macmillan, who is said to be in ill-heath and whose party has been dogged by scandal, resigns.

Oct 18th   The 1968 Summer Olympics are awarded to Mexico City after a meeting of the International Olympic Committee in Baden Baden, West Germany.

Oct 28th   Belfast Aldergrove opens as the main airport for Northern Ireland. The previous main airport at Nutts Corner is closed.

Nov 1st   Indigenous Australians win the right to vote in Federal Elections in Western Australia, Northern Territory and Queensland. This brings them into line with other states where indigenous voting rights have been in place since 1949.

Nov 2nd   Rebels surround the Presidential Palace in Saigon, Vietnam. After two hours of constant shelling, the guards inside the palace raise the white flag. When the rebels enter the palace they find that the President, Ngo Dinh Diem and his brother Ngo Dinh Nhu have fled. They are tracked down to a local beauty parlour and then beaten and shot.

Nov 2nd   President John F. Kennedy who is scheduled to travel in a motorcade in Chicago to watch the annual Army vs Navy football game, cancels the tour in order to address the crisis in Vietnam.

Nov 8th   Prime Minister Alec Douglas-Home, who as the 14th Earl of Home, had been leading the country from the House of Lords, wins the Kinross and Western Perth by-election after renouncing his peerage.

Nov 18th   The Bell Telephone Company introduces the first touch-tone telephone to its customers in Pennsylvania.

Nov 21st   President John F. Kennedy flies to Texas.

Nov 22nd   Shots are fired at a motorcade carrying Kennedy, his wife Jacqueline and several senior government officials through the streets of Dallas. Kennedy is hit and is rushed to hospital, but is pronounced dead shortly after arrival. The shocking news reverberates around the globe. Lee Harvey Oswald is arrested for the murder. Vice President Lyndon B. Johnson is sworn in as President.

Nov 24th   Whilst being escorted by police to an armoured car, Lee Harvey Oswald is shot and murdered by nightclub owner Jack Ruby, who claims he is grief-stricken "to the point of insanity" over the assassination of JFK.

Nov 25th   Kennedy is laid to rest at Arlington National Cemetery after a service at St. Matthew's Cathedral. In attendance are leaders from around the world. Britain is represented by Prime Minister, Alec Douglas-Home. Also present are President Charles de Gaulle from France, Ethiopian Emperor Haile Selassie and Irish President Éamon de Valera.

Nov 29th   President Johnson establishes the Warren Commission to investigate JFK's assassination.

Dec 1st   Malcolm X describes the Kennedy assassination as a case of America's "chickens coming home to roost". This results in his suspension and subsequent excommunication from the nation of Islam.

Dec 3rd   Italy reduces the size of its banknotes, which had been referred to as "bed sheet" size because each bill was almost 25cm by 12cm (almost 10in long by 5in wide). The new size of the Lira, 15cm by 7.5cm (almost 6in by 3in) is a little more than one-third as large in total area, and closer in size to other world currencies.

Dec 4th   The United Nations Security Council unanimously (11 to 0) adopts resolution 182 condemning the apartheid policy of the Government of the Republic of South Africa.

Dec 5th   The new game Mouse Trap is in the toy shops in time for Christmas. It is one of the first mass-produced three-dimensional board games. Players must co-operate to build a working mousetrap. Then, players turn against each other to trap opponents' mouse-shaped game pieces.

Dec 6th   Two weeks after the assassination of President Kennedy, former First Lady Jacqueline Kennedy and her children move out of the White House. New President Johnson and his wife Lady Bird had agreed that the Kennedy family could have as much time as they needed to find a new home.

Dec 7th   Tony Vema, a CBS director, invents the concept of "Instant Replay" during a live broadcast of football's annual Army vs Navy game. In the fourth quarter, Army quarterback Rollie Stichweh runs for a touchdown. Within seconds, technicians rewind the black and white videotape, then play the recording back on television. Commentator Lindsey Nelson tells viewers "This is not live. Ladies and gentlemen, Army did not score again!"

Dec 7th   Americans get their first glimpse of the new British music group, The Beatles, when a clip of one of their performances is shown on the CBS Evening News. Radio stations in the U.S. begin to receive requests to play Beatles songs, and several shops begin to import copies from the U.K.

Dec 8th   Frank Sinatra Jr., the 19-year-old son of the renowned singer, is kidnapped. The kidnappers demand a ransom of $240,000. Frank's Jr.'s father pays the ransom and the kidnap victim is released.

Dec 10th   6-year-old Donny Osmond makes his TV debut on *The Andy Williams Show*.

Dec 21st   The Daleks are featured in *Dr. Who* for the first time. In the episode *The Dead Planet*, the Doctor and his three companions arrive in the TARDIS on the planet Skaro, although viewers would not see what a Dalek looked like until the December 28th episode.

Dec 22nd   The official 30-day mourning period for President John F. Kennedy draws to an end.

Dec 25th   The Queen decides that her Christmas Broadcast in 1963 should be done by broadcast on radio as she is pregnant with her fourth child. In it she addresses the nation and states:

"Since my last message of Christmas greetings to you all, the world has witnessed many great events and sweeping changes, but they are already part of the long record of history. Now, as ever, the important time for mankind is the future; the coming years are full of hope and promise and their course can still be shaped by our will and action. The message of Christmas remains the same; but humanity can only progress if we are all truly ambitious for what is good and honourable."

 ## José Mário dos Santos Mourinho Félix GOIH
born on 26th January 1963 in Setúbal, Portugal

Once dubbed "The Special One" by the British media, Mourinho is one of the most decorated managers ever and is widely considered to be among the greatest managers of all time. There is a saying in football that great players never make great managers and Mourinho bears this out. He was a very average player who played in the lower leagues of Portuguese football. His big break came when he was hired as as an interpreter for English manager Bobby Robson at Sporting CP and Porto. He would later take over at Porto and lead them to victory in the Champions League in 2002. It is probably easier to list the trophies Mourinho hasn't won throughout his career. He has delivered success at every club he has managed except for a brief spell at Tottenham Hotspur. His two spells at Chelsea saw him win three Premier League titles. He led Inter Milan to Champions League glory and he guided Manchester United to Europa League victory. In 2022, under his tutelage, Roma won the Europa Conference League, making Mourinho the only manager to win all three of European football's current major trophies. His intense and confrontational style has led him to fall out with fellow managers, directors and even players with his tenure at clubs rarely lasting long. However, the fans at each club he has managed have remained almost universally loyal, forgiving him his foibles and revelling in the success he has delivered.

Paul Whitehouse created the character Jose Arrogantio, a brilliant send-up of Mourinho, in the series *Harry and Paul*.

 ## Michael Jeffrey Jordan
born on 17th February 1963 in Brooklyn, New York, USA

Michael Jordan is widely considered one of the greatest basketball players of all time. Though born in the Big Apple he grew up in Wilmington, North Carolina. He played college basketball at the University of North Carolina, where he won a national championship in 1982. In 1984, he was drafted by the Chicago Bulls as the third overall pick (the two players picked above him were Nigerian Hakeem Olajuwon and Pennsylvanian Sam Browne). Jordan quickly established himself as a dominant force in the NBA, earning Rookie of the Year honours in his first season. He was known for his incredible athleticism, leaping ability and speed. He also had exceptional shooting and scoring skills. Over the course of his career, Jordan won six NBA championships with the Bulls, earning five NBA Most Valuable Player awards and ten scoring titles. He was also a 14-time NBA All-Star and won two Olympic gold medals with the US men's basketball team. His ability to rise to the occasion and deliver in high-pressure situations earned him the nickname "Air Jordan." He retired from the NBA three times, but continued to make an impact on the sport through his ownership of the Charlotte Hornets and his influence on the game as a cultural icon.

He began his first comeback season on the court with the Washington Wizards in September 2001. After that month's terrorist attack on the Twin Towers he donated his entire salary to victims' charities.

🎵 Seal Henry Olusegun Olumide Adeola Samuel
born on 19th February 1963 in Paddington, London, UK

Seal was raised in foster care for a time before being brought up by his stepmother and father, who was a difficult and angry figure. Despite this turbulent upbringing, he gained a degree in architecture and then worked in various jobs. By the time he was 23, he had developed scars on his face as the result of a rare form of lupus. His first foray into music was singing in local bars which lead him to working with the funk band Push where he toured to Japan, Thailand and India in 1987. Seal's big breakthrough onto the music scene came in 1990 when he collaborated with producer Adamski on the number one song, *Killer*. He made his full-length, self-titled album debut in 1991 and scored with the moody, socially aware single *Crazy*, which reached the Top 10 of Billboard's pop chart. He won several British awards and released his second self-titled album in 1994, a work that was musically more lush than its predecessor and featured *Prayer Before Dying* and *Don't Cry*, as well as vocals from Joni Mitchell. Another single, *Kiss From a Rose*, featured on the soundtrack to *Batman Forever* and became a No. 1 hit catapulting him to multi-platinum status. He went on to win Grammys for Record of the Year, Song of the Year and Best Male Pop Vocal Performance. In the autumn of 2008, Seal released *Soul*, a collection of covers featuring the works of R&B greats like Ben E. King, Curtis Mayfield and Otis Redding.

Alluding to his difficult childhood Seal stated "I believe that in all forms of art there has to have been some initial adversity: that is what makes art, as far as I'm concerned."

🎬 Quentin Jerome Tarantino
born on 27th March 1963 in Knoxville, Tennessee, USA

Quentin Tarantino is an American filmmaker, screenwriter and actor, known for his unique and unconventional approach to filmmaking. He wrote and directed his first feature film, *Reservoir Dogs* in 1992. The film quickly gained critical acclaim for its innovative narrative structure, non-linear storytelling, stylised violence, references to other movies and sharp dialogue. Tarantino continued his success with the release of *Pulp Fiction* (1994), which won the Palme d'Or at the Cannes Film Festival and earned seven Academy Award nominations, winning Best Original Screenplay. Throughout his career, Tarantino has become known for his unique directorial style, which blends elements of exploitation, spaghetti westerns and film noir. Some of his other notable films include *Kill Bill Volumes 1 and 2* (2003, 2004), *Inglourious Basterds* (2009), *Django Unchained* (2012) and *Once Upon a Time in Hollywood* (2019). Tarantino has received numerous awards throughout his career, including two Academy Awards for Best Original Screenplay. He is also known for his collaborations with actors such as Uma Thurman and Samuel L. Jackson. Although Tarantino is most at ease behind the camera, like Hitchcock and Scorsese, he has made several cameo appearances in his movies. His unique style and influence on cinema have made him one of the most celebrated and controversial filmmakers of his generation.

Tarantino often creates fictional brands of objects due to his dislike of product placement. The Red Apple cigarettes and Big Kahuna burger established in Pulp Fiction are often referenced in his other films.

Graham William Walker aka Graham Norton
born on 4th April 1963 in Clondalkin, County Dublin, Ireland

Graham Norton is an Irish comedian, actor, author and television host, known for his witty humour and lively personality. Norton began his career as a stand-up comedian, performing in comedy clubs and theatres throughout the UK and Ireland. He later moved into television, hosting various talk shows, game shows and awards ceremonies. In 1998, he landed his own talk show, *So Graham Norton*, on Channel 4, which became a hit and ran for six series. He later hosted *The Graham Norton Show* on BBC 2, which aired from 2007 to 2009 and then moved to BBC 1. The show has featured celebrity interviews, musical performances and comedic skits. In addition to his talk show, Norton has also hosted various game shows, including *Bring Me the Head of Light Entertainment* and *The Generation Game*. In 2009 he took over as British host of the *Eurovision Song Contest* from Terry Wogan and brought it kicking and screaming into the 21st century, He has written several acclaimed books, including his autobiography, *So Me* and the novel *Holding*. He has also acted in various films and television shows, including *Father Ted*, *Absolutely Fabulous: The Movie* and an uncredited appearance in the soap opera *Brookside*.

In December 2001, the first ever talking waxwork was unveiled at Madame Tussaud's London museum featuring a Graham Norton replica as the lifelike figurine. Visitors were offered three options of Norton's impudent catchphrases: innocent innuendos, cheeky banter, or X-rated doubles entendres.

Garry Kimovich Kasparov
born on 13th April 1963 in Baku, Azerbaijan SSR, Soviet Union

Kasparov is a retired Azerbaijani-Russian chess player widely regarded as one of the greatest players in the history of the game. He learned to play chess at a young age and began competing in tournaments as a child. In 1985, at the age of 22, he became the youngest ever undisputed World Chess Champion, a title he held for 15 years until he was defeated by Vladimir Kramnik in 2000. He also held the FIDE World Chess Championship title from 1993 to 2000. Kasparov's playing style was aggressive and strategic and he was known for his ability to think several moves ahead of his opponents.

He was particularly successful in rapid and blitz chess, winning numerous championships in both formats. In addition to his success on the chessboard, Kasparov was also a vocal political activist advocating for democracy and human rights in Russia. He retired from professional chess in 2005 and has since written several books on the game, as well as on politics and technology. Kasparov's legacy in chess is significant, with many of his games and strategies still studied and admired by players today.

In 1996 Kasparov played against an IBM supercomputer called Deep Blue in Philadelphia. It was a contest that captured the world's imagination. Kasparov won the best-of-six contest 4-2. A re-match was held the following year in New York, this time Deep Blue won 3½ to 2½. It was the subject of a documentary film, *Game Over: Kasparov and the Machine*.

Natasha Jane Richardson
born on 11th May 1963 in Marylebone, London, UK

Richardson spent much of her life being labelled, firstly as the daughter of Vanessa Redgrave and then as the wife of Liam Neeson. She tried hard to throw off what she called "the family baggage" and carved out a career for herself on stage and in film. She made her debut at the age of four, playing a flower girl in her father Tony Richardson's 1968 film *The Charge of the Light Brigade*, which also featured her mother Vanessa and uncle Corin Redgrave. She later acknowledged that her father had the most influence on her as an actress. "His faith in me gave me a sense of belief in myself" she said.

Her first UK television role was in the acclaimed Granada production of *The Adventures of Sherlock Holmes*. Her career received a boost in 1990 when she appeared as Offred in the science fiction film *A Handmaid's Tale* with Faye Dunaway and Robert Duvall. She starred with Jodie Foster in the 1994 film *Nell* where she found herself working with Neeson. The couple married the same year. It was back to the stage in 1998 where she won a Tony for her portrayal of Sally Bowles in a New York stage revival of the musical *Cabaret*. In 2005, she again appeared in a New York theatrical revival, this time as Blanche Dubois in *A Streetcar Named Desire*.

Tragically, in 2009, she died following a skiing accident in Canada. The lights on Broadway were dimmed in her honour.

John Christopher Depp II aka Johnny Depp
born on 9th June 1963 in Owensboro, Kentucky, USA

Johnny Depp is a highly acclaimed American actor, producer and musician known for his versatility and chameleon-like ability to inhabit a wide range of characters in film and television. Depp began his acting career in the 1980s with small roles in various films and television shows. He gained widespread recognition in 1987 for his role in the television series *21 Jump Street*, where he played an undercover police officer. In the 1990s, Depp became a major Hollywood star, thanks to his iconic roles in films such as *Edward Scissorhands*, *Sleepy Hollow*, *What's Eating Gilbert Grape* and *Pirates of the Caribbean*. Depp has received numerous awards and nominations for his work, including three Academy Award nominations, seven Golden Globe nominations, and a Screen Actors Guild Award. He is also known for his collaborations with renowned director Tim Burton, with whom he has worked on numerous films. In addition to his acting career, Depp is an accomplished musician and has been involved in several musical projects, including forming the rock supergroup Hollywood Vampires with Alice Cooper and Joe Perry. He has also accompanied his good friend, guitar legend Jeff Beck, on tour.

Depp lists British comedy *The Fast Show*, renamed *Brilliant* for American television, as his favourite television program of all time. He would take tapes of the series on tour with him to keep him amused. He made a guest appearance in the last-ever sketch. "Suits You Sir." in its last ever episode.

Georgios Kyriacos Panayiotou aka George Michael
born on 25th June 1963 in East Finchley, Middlesex, UK

George Michael was a British singer, songwriter and producer who rose to fame in the 1980s as a member of the pop duo Wham! and later as a successful solo artist. Michael's music career began in 1982 when he and his friend Andrew Ridgeley formed Wham!. The duo's debut album, *Fantastic*, was released in 1983 and produced several hit singles, including *Young Guns (Go for It)* and *Club Tropicana*. Wham! became one of the most successful pop acts of the 1980s, with a string of chart-topping hits including *Wake Me Up Before You Go-Go* and *Last Christmas*. After Wham! disbanded in 1986, Michael pursued a successful solo career, releasing a string of hit albums, including *Faith* (1987) which sold over 25 million copies worldwide. Michael's solo hits included *Careless Whisper*, *Father Figure* and *Freedom! '90*. Throughout his career, Michael was known for his soulful voice, his songwriting abilities and his social activism. He was a strong supporter of minority rights, frequently using his music to speak out against social injustice. Michael's untimely death at the age of 53 shocked fans around the world. Elton John paid tribute by saying: "What a singer, what a songwriter. But more than anything, as a human being, he was one of the kindest, sweetest, most generous people I've ever met."

Michael was known for his random acts of kindness, most of which were only revealed after his death. He worked at a homeless shelter in London. He funded a woman's IVF treatment after watching an episode of *Fifteen-to-One*, where a contestant explained her reason for being on the show. He also donated £50,000 to send deprived children to Lapland.

Tracey Karima Emin CBE RA
born on 3rd July 1963 in Croydon, South London, UK

Emin is a contemporary British artist who is widely known for her confessional and autobiographical artworks that explore themes of love, sex, loss and trauma, She grew up in a working-class family and endured a difficult childhood marked by abuse and neglect. Her early experiences have greatly influenced her artistic style and subject matter. She is best known for her installations, which often feature a variety of mixed media such as neon lights, drawings, sculptures and personal items. One of her most iconic works is *My Bed* (1998), which consisted of her own unmade bed surrounded by personal items such as cigarettes, condoms and a vodka bottle. The piece caused controversy when it was shortlisted for the Turner Prize, one of the UK's most prestigious art awards.

Emin's work is often deeply personal exposing her vulnerabilities, struggles and emotions. Her art is also infused with a feminist sensibility that challenges traditional gender roles and societal norms. Many of her works explore the female body, sexuality and desire, such as her series of embroidered blankets and neon light sculptures that feature provocative phrases.

My Bed became the most viewed piece of art in the UK in 1999. Thousands queued up to view it when it went on display at the Tate gallery in London. This number was dwarfed by the millions who viewed it when it appeared, as part of an article mocking it, on the front page of The Sun newspaper.

Marco Giuseppe Salussolia aka Mark Strong
born on 5th August 1963 in London, UK

Mark Strong is an accomplished British actor who has made a name for himself on stage, television and film. He began his career in the early 1990s, working primarily on stage. He quickly gained recognition for his work, earning critical acclaim for his performances in plays such as *Death of a Salesman* and *A View from the Bridge*. His first major television role was as Terry "Tosker" Cox in the BBC's *Our Friends in the North*, alongside Daniel Craig, Christopher Ecclestone and Gina McKee. In the late 1990s, he began to transition into film, appearing in small roles in movies like *Emma* and *Elephant Juice*. His big cinematic breakthrough role came in 2005 with his portrayal of crime boss Frank D'Amico in the film *Kick-Ass*. He has since become known for his portrayals of villains and antagonists, including the roles of Prince Septimus in *Stardust*, Lord Blackwood in *Sherlock Holmes* and Hani Salaam in *Body of Lies*. He has also appeared in a variety of other films, including *Tinker Tailor Soldier Spy*, *Kingsman: The Secret Service*, *The Imitation Game* and *1917*. Strong is a lifelong Arsenal FC fan. He lives in London with his family and is a close friend of Daniel Craig. In fact, Craig is the godfather of Strong's son Roman.

On working with Christopher Ecclestone in *Our Friends in the North*, Strong stated: "He didn't speak to me for the whole year we were filming. At first I thought it was to do with the characters, because there was supposed to be tension between us, but then I realised he just didn't like me."

Whitney Elizabeth Houston
born on 9th August 1963 in Newark, New Jersey, USA

Houston was born into music. Her mother, Cissy, was a renowned gospel singer and her cousin was none other than Dione Warwick. She started her music career in the 1980s soon becoming one of the most successful female singers of the decade with hits such as *How Will I Know*, *Saving All My Love for You* and *I Wanna Dance with Somebody*. During her career, Houston sold over 200 million records worldwide, making her one of the best-selling music artists of all time. She also won numerous awards, including six Grammys, two Emmys and thirty Billboard Music Awards. In addition to her music career, Houston acted in several films, including *The Bodyguard* and *Waiting to Exhale*. Despite her incredible talent and success, Houston struggled with addiction and personal issues throughout her life. She was married to singer Bobby Brown for several years. The couple had a tumultuous relationship that was all too often in the public eye. Houston's drug use and erratic behaviour eventually began to affect her career. She died in 2012, at the age of 48, due to accidental drowning in her hotel room bathtub with the effects of heart disease and cocaine use as contributing factors. Houston is widely acknowledged as a cultural icon and one of the most exceptional vocalists ever. Moreover, she holds a distinguished position as one of the most influential R&B artists in history.

When *Where Do Broken Hearts Go* hit #1 in April 1988, she became the first artist in history to ever have seven consecutive Billboard number one singles.

🎵 Jarvis Branson Cocker
born on 19th September 1963 in Sheffield, Yorkshire, UK

Jarvis Cocker is an English musician, singer-songwriter and frontman of the band Pulp. Cocker formed the band in 1978 with his schoolmates. They released their first album in 1983, but it wasn't until the mid-1990s that they achieved mainstream success with hits like *Common People* and *Disco 2000*. Cocker's distinctive vocals and witty lyrics quickly made him a cult figure in the Britpop scene, somewhat aloof from the main protagonists Blur and Oasis. He is known for his often tongue-in-cheek commentary on British society and his sharp sense of humour. His onstage antics, including his iconic dance moves, elevated his performance into an art form. In addition to his work with Pulp, Cocker has released several solo albums, including *Jarvis* in 2006 and *Further Complications* in 2009. He has also collaborated with other musicians and artists, such as Nancy Sinatra and Chilly Gonzales. Cocker is also a well-respected radio presenter, hosting shows on BBC Radio 6 Music and Radio 4. He has presented television documentaries on subjects such as outsider art and the history of music in Sheffield. Throughout his career, Cocker has been noted for his intelligent and thought-provoking lyrics, his unique voice and the ability to capture the zeitgeist of British society.

The song *Common People* is autobiographical. Cocker did study at St. Martins College. The woman in the video "who came from Greece with a thirst for knowledge" is none other than the actress, Sadie Frost.

🎬 Wendell Edward Pierce
born on 8th December 1963 in New Orleans, Louisiana, USA

Pierce's mother was a teacher and his father was a decorated World War II veteran, who in civilian life worked as a maintenance engineer. His father's segregated army unit helped the US Marines win the Battle of Saipan in 1944. Pierce said of his father's experience: "My father fought in World War II and loved this country when this country wasn't loving him back." Although not strictly a method actor, he had a method in his acting career. Each year he aimed to do one film, one TV series and one play. The pinnacle of his TV career came when he played Detective Bunk Moreland in HBO's *The Wire*. He also played high-powered attorney Robert Zane in *Suits* alongside Meghan Markle. He had parts in the films *Malcolm X* and *Waiting to Exhale*, but perhaps his finest performance was when he played the lead role of Willy Lomax in a revival of *Death of a Salesman* in 2019 at the Piccadilly Theatre in London. He also reached a global audience in his leading role as James Greer in Amazon Prime's political action thriller series *Jack Ryan*. Outside of acting, Pierce is socially active. In December 2011, noticing that there were few places to buy fresh produce in his native New Orleans, he opened Sterling Express, a chain of stores bringing healthy goods to the city.

After losing his childhood home to Hurricane Katrina in 2005, Wendell suffered yet another devastating loss in August 2016 when another home was taken from him due to widespread flooding in Louisiana. The flooding was almost 11 years to the day after Katrina made landfall.

William Bradley Pitt
born on 18th December 1963 in Shawnee, Oklahoma, USA

Brad Pitt is an American actor and producer. He rose to fame in the early 1990s with roles in films such as *Thelma & Louise* and *A River Runs Through It*. Since then, he has become one of the most recognisable and successful actors in Hollywood. Pitt has received numerous awards and nominations throughout his career, including an Academy Award for Best Supporting Actor for his role in *Once Upon a Time in Hollywood*. He has also been nominated for three additional Academy Awards, five Golden Globe Awards and three BAFTA Awards. In addition to his acting career, Pitt is also a successful film producer. He co-founded the production company Plan B Entertainment, which has produced several critically acclaimed films, including *12 Years a Slave*, *Moonlight* and *The Big Short*. He is also known for his high-profile relationships, including his marriage to Jennifer Aniston and his later relationship with Angelina Jolie. He has six children, three of whom are adopted. Despite his fame and success, Pitt is known for his down-to-earth personality and his philanthropic efforts. He has been involved in various charitable efforts throughout his career, including environmental and humanitarian causes.

Pitt has appeared in three movies with the number seven in the title: *Seven* (1995), *Seven Years in Tibet* (1997) and *Sinbad: Legend of the Seven Seas* (2003). He has also appeared in three films with twelve in the title – *Twelve Monkeys* (1995), *Ocean's Twelve* (2004) and *12 Years a Slave* (2013).

Other Notable Births

James May
16th January 1963
Presenter | Journalist

George Monbiot
27th January 1963
Writer | Activist

Vanessa Williams
18th March 1963
Actress | Singer

Peter Jones
18th March 1963
Entrepreneur | Presenter

David Thewlis
20th March 1963
Actor | Author

Mike Myers
25th May 1963
Actor | Comedian

Jason Isaacs
6th June 1963
Actor

Helen Hunt
15th June 1963
Actress | Director

Norman Cook
16th July 1963
DJ | Producer

Lisa Kudrow
30th July 1963
Actress | Producer

Emmanuelle Béart
14th August 1963
Actress

Sanjeev Bhaskar
31st October 1963
Actor | Comedian

Johnny Marr
31st October 1963
Musician | Singer

Ian Wright
3rd November 1963
Footballer | Presenter

Hugh Bonneville
10th November 1963
Actor

His Journey to becoming President

Born soon after America's entry into the First World War, John Fitzgerald Kennedy was to become the nation's first president born in the 20th century. Both of his parents hailed from wealthy Bostonian families with long political histories. Kennedy's father, Joseph P. Kennedy, had made a fortune in the stock market, entertainment and other business, managing to take his money out of the stock market just before the crash of 1929. Though the ensuing Great Depression gripped the nation, John and his eight siblings enjoyed a

The Kennedy family in 1931 (JFK top left)

privileged childhood of elite private schools, servants and summer homes. Kennedy later claimed that his only experience of the Great Depression came from what he read in books while attending Harvard University. However, for all the privilege John's childhood was interrupted repeatedly by bouts of chronic illness. Afflicted with an almost constant stream of ailments, several of which went undiagnosed, Kennedy spent much of his time recuperating. In 1938, on the eve of the Second World War, President Roosevelt appointed John's father to the key post of ambassador to the United

Kingdom. The new ambassador was unsympathetic to British preparedness policies and found a cool reception in London. That year, John inherited $1 million dollars from his family, but his ambition remained strong. While in England with his father, he wrote his senior essay for Harvard University on England's lack of readiness for the Second World War. It was published and was well received by critics, becoming a bestseller under the title *Why England Slept*. After Kennedy graduated from Harvard, the United States entered World War II. His efforts to join the US Navy were initially thwarted by his ill-health, but after his father intervened, he was eventually admitted and assigned to serve in the South Pacific, commanding a small motor-torpedo boat known as a "PT boat". Kennedy and his crew participated in the campaign to recapture thousands of islands from

Kennedy on board his PT-109 torpedo boat

Japanese control. When the boat he commanded collided with the Japanese destroyer Amagiri in August 1943, he led the ten surviving men to safety, swimming for three miles to a tiny island. He returned home a much-decorated hero. After being discharged from the Navy, John Kennedy worked briefly as a reporter for Hearst newspapers. In 1946, the twenty-nine-year-old Kennedy won election to the US Congress representing a working-class Boston district. He served three terms in the US House of Representatives, earning a

The Kennedy's wedding on 12th September 1953

reputation as a somewhat conservative Democrat. In 1952, he successfully ran for the US Senate, defeating Henry Cabot Lodge Jr., the Republican incumbent from another Massachusetts family with a long political history. That same year, he met Jacqueline Bouvier at a dinner party and, as he later put it, "leaned across the asparagus and asked her for a date." The two were married a year later and had three children, one of whom died in infancy in August 1963. In 1956 Kennedy ran for the Democrat nomination for Presidential candidate. It was the most inauspicious of starts as he gained only 969 votes out of over 6 million. In 1960, he was more successful beating Lyndon B Johnson in the primaries and then Richard Nixon in the Presidential elections to become the 35th President of The United States.

His Death

John F. Kennedy was assassinated on 22nd November 1963, while riding in an open-top car through the streets of Dallas, Texas. The assassination was a traumatic event that shocked the world, and has been the subject of much speculation and controversy ever since. Kennedy's motorcade was moving slowly through Dealey Plaza when shots rang out, hitting the President in the head and neck. He was rushed to a nearby hospital but was pronounced dead soon after his arrival. The assassination was captured on film by numerous bystanders and the footage has been studied and analysed extensively in the years since. The investigation into Kennedy's assassination was led by the Warren Commission, which was established by

Official presidential portrait from July 1963

President Lyndon B. Johnson shortly after the assassination. The Commission concluded that Lee Harvey Oswald, a former Marine who had defected to the Soviet Union and later returned to the United States, acted alone in shooting Kennedy from a sixth-floor window of the Texas School Book Depository building. However, the Warren Commission's findings have been the subject of controversy and scepticism from the beginning. Many people have questioned whether Oswald acted alone, or whether there was a larger conspiracy involving multiple individuals or organisations. Some have even suggested that the assassination was orchestrated by the CIA or other government agencies. The fact that Oswald himself was killed just two days after Kennedy's assassination only added to the sense of mystery and suspicion surrounding the events in Dallas. Jack Ruby, a nightclub owner with ties to organised crime, shot Oswald in the basement of the Dallas police headquarters while he

Moments before the shooting

was being transferred to another facility. Over the years, a number of investigations and inquiries have been conducted into the Kennedy assassination, including the House Select Committee on Assassinations in the 1970s. This committee concluded that Kennedy was likely killed as the result of a conspiracy, although it did not identify any specific individuals or groups responsible. Despite the many investigations and inquiries, the assassination of John F. Kennedy remains one of the most controversial and debated events in American history. The lack of definitive answers or closure has fuelled endless speculation and countless conspiracy theories, and it is likely that the debate will continue for many years to come.

Lee Harvey Oswald in custody

Hugh Todd Naylor Gaitskell CBE
died aged 56 on 18th January 1963 in London, UK

Hugh Gaitskell was born in 1906 in Kensington, London. He was a British politician and leader of the Labour Party from 1955 until his death in 1963. He was known for his efforts to modernise the party and shift it away from its socialist roots towards a more centrist position. He studied at Oxford University before entering politics. He was elected to Parliament in 1945 and quickly rose through the ranks of the Labour Party, serving in various positions including Minister of Fuel and Power and Chancellor of the Exchequer. He advocated for a more market-based economy and closer ties with the United States. His tenure was cut short by his sudden death, but his ideas and legacy continued to influence British politics. He is remembered as a key figure in the transformation of the Labour Party from a socialist movement to a more pragmatic and centrist political force and is often described as "the best Prime Minister we never had."

Robert Lee Frost
died aged 88 on 29th January 1963 in Boston, Massachusetts, USA

Frost is considered one of the most pre-eminent and influential poets of the 20th century. His poetry often focused on rural life in New England where he spent much of his life. His writing style was characterised by his use of colloquial language and his ability to convey complex themes through simple, accessible imagery. Many of his poems deal with universal themes such as love, loss and the human condition. Some of his most famous works include *The Road Not Taken*, *Stopping by Woods on a Snowy Evening* and *Mending Wall*. These poems have become staples of American literature and are still taught in schools to this day. In addition to his poetry, Frost was also a teacher and lecturer. He received many honours during his life, including four Pulitzer Prizes, a record for a poet. In 1961, two years before his death, he was appointed Poet Laureate of Vermont.

Sylvia Plath
died aged 30 on 11th February 1963 in London, UK

Sylvia Plath was an American poet, novelist and short-story writer. Her work was characterised by its intense, raw emotional content, as well as its strikingly vivid and often disturbing imagery. Plath's most famous work was her semi-autobiographical novel, *The Bell Jar*, which details the mental breakdown of a young woman in the 1950s. Her poetry is renowned for its powerful evocation of personal turmoil and its intricate use of language. Her most famous poetry collection, *Ariel*, was published posthumously in 1965 and is widely regarded as a masterpiece of confessional poetry. Plath's work often dealt with themes of suicide, depression and the struggle for personal identity. Tragically, she took her own life at the age of 30. *The Collected Poems* was published in 1981, which included previously unpublished works. For this collection she was awarded a Pulitzer Prize in 1982, making her only the fourth person to receive the honour posthumously.

🎵 Édith Piaf
died aged 47 on 10th October 1963 in Paris, France

Piaf, born in 1915, was a French singer and songwriter who became an icon of French popular music. Growing up in Paris, she had a difficult childhood marked by poverty, illness and the loss of her mother at an early age. She began singing on Paris streets as a teenager and was discovered by a nightclub owner, who gave her a start in the music industry. Piaf's distinctive voice and emotional performances made her an instant success and she went on to become the most influential French singer of her time. She sang a wide range of songs, from upbeat cabaret tunes to heartbreaking ballads. Piaf also wrote many of her own songs. Her life was marked by personal struggles, including numerous unhappy love affairs, drug addiction and health problems. Her greatest song *Non, je ne regrette rien* (No, I regret nothing) is one of the most popular funeral songs in France. It covers similar themes to the most popular funeral song in the UK, *My Way*.

📖 Aldous Leonard Huxley
died aged 69 on 22nd November 1963 in Los Angeles County, USA

Aldous Huxley was an English writer and philosopher. He is perhaps best known for his dystopian novel, *Brave New World*, which was published in 1932 and which is still widely read today. He was born into an intellectual family and was well-educated from a young age. He studied at Oxford University and later worked as a teacher and journalist. Throughout his life, he was interested in the big questions of human existence and was a prolific writer on a wide range of topics, including philosophy, psychology, spirituality and politics. In addition to *Brave New World*, Huxley wrote many other works of fiction and non-fiction, including *The Doors of Perception*, *Island* and *The Perennial Philosophy*. He was a leading thinker of his time and his ideas continue to influence contemporary culture and society. Huxley was known for his scepticism of modern society and its values, and he believed that the key to a fulfilling life was to seek knowledge and understanding of oneself and the world.

📖 Clive Staples Lewis aka C.S.Lewis
died aged 64 on 22nd November 1963 in Oxford, England

Clive Staples Lewis, born in Belfast in 1898, commonly known as C.S. Lewis, was a British writer and scholar. He is best known for his works of fiction including *The Chronicles of Narnia* series and *The Space Trilogy*, as well as his non-fiction works on religion. He attended Oxford University and subsequently became a professor of English literature at both Oxford and Cambridge. He was a close friend of J.R.R. Tolkien, author of *The Lord of the Rings* series. He was also part of a literary group in Oxford known as The Inklings. Lewis was a prolific writer, producing works in a variety of genres including science fiction, literary criticism, theology and poetry. His Christian faith was a central theme in much of his writing, and he is considered one of the most influential lay thinkers of the 20th century. Lewis's legacy as a writer and Christian philosopher continues to influence and inspire readers around the world.

The Coins We Used

8 years before decimalisation, the United Kingdom used the system of **pounds**, **shillings** and **pence**, commonly represented using the symbols **£sd**. The **£** symbol evolved over many years from the letter **L** which derives from the Latin word *libra*, meaning a pound of money. Although **s** is the first letter of the word shilling, the use of the letter derives from the Latin word *solidus*, which means coin. The curious use of the letter **d** for pennies also has a Latin origin from the word *denarius*, meaning containing ten.

Unlike the decimal system based on multiples of 10, the pre-decimal system was based on multiples of 12. There were 12 pennies to a shilling and 240 pennies to a pound. This meant there were 20 shillings to the pound. In 1963 there were 8 coins in circulation with evocative names that still permeate our language today. Note: The farthing (¼ d) ceased to be legal tender 2 years earlier in 1961.

	Coin	Description
	Halfpenny ½ d *In use to 1969*	Commonly known as the *ha'penny* it is was the only word in the English language with a silent 'f'. Since 1937 the coin featured Sir Francis Drake's ship The Golden Hind. The popular pub game *Shove Ha'penny* features 5 halfpennies.
	Penny 1d *In use to 1971*	Before 1860 the penny was a large copper coin. This is why bicycles with a large front wheel were nicknamed Penny Farthings. Popular expressions using the penny include *ten a penny* and *a penny for your thoughts*.
	Threepence 3d *In use to 1971*	These 12-sided coins were commonly known as *thruppence* or *thrupenny bits*. The silver versions known as *joeys* were often hidden in Christmas puddings making an exciting find for the lucky children who discovered them.
	Sixpence 6d *In use to 1980*	These silver coins reputedly brought good luck. Sixpences were placed in bride's shoes as a wedding gesture. Known as benders, they could easily be bent. *Going on a bender* derived from drinking all day in pubs with sixpence.
	Shilling 1/- *In use to 1990*	First minted in the reign of Henry VII as a testoon, the shilling was latterly commonly known as a bob. *Taking the king's shilling* meant enrolling in the army whilst *a few bob short of a pound* describes someone a bit dim.
	Florin 2/- *In use to 1992*	The florin was Britain's first decimal coin in response to calls in the mid 19th Century for decimal coinage to be introduced. As 2 bob, the florin was worth 1/10th of a pound. After decimalisation in 1971, florins became worth 10 pence.
	Half Crown 2/6 *In use to 1969*	Half crowns were originally struck in gold in the reign of Henry VIII. The first silver half crowns were issued under Edward VI in 1549. Surviving for over 450 years, the half crown was one of the most successful coins of all time.
	Crown 5/- *In use to present day*	The British crown is a heavy silver coin. Rarely spent, crowns are often minted for commemorative purposes. After decimalisation a crown was worth 25p until 1990 when their face value was changed to £5.

The average annual wage in the UK in 1963 was approximately:

£850-£900

The Mark I Ford Cortina was launched in the UK in 1962. Originally to be named the Ford Consul 225, the car was launched as the Consul Cortina until a facelift in 1964 when the Consul name was dropped. The 50hp standard model would go from 0-60 in 22.5 seconds using its 1198 cc, 4 cylinder engine. Base model prices started at:

£600

The price of the average house would be approximately 3-5x the average annual wage. Depending on where you were in the country this meant the price of a typical 1930's 3-bedroom semi-detached house would be in the region of:

£2,500 - £3,000

The Olympia Splendid 33 portable manual typewriter cost:

£24

In 1963 the average cost for a pint of milk would have been:

8½d

A gallon of petrol (which is equivalent to 4.5 litres) cost:

5s

Working Overseas

"Ten Pound Poms" en route to Australia on-board SS New Australia

At work on a rubber plantation in Malaysia

The ten pound assisted passage scheme to Australia proved extremely popular, with two clear waves of migration occurring firstly in the immediate post-war period, and then peaking in the 1960s. These 'Ten Pound Poms', as they became known (82% were English), were mostly from an urban background and were motivated by various factors: to escape post-war austerity, to take advantage of a warmer climate and an outdoor lifestyle, or to fulfil a sense of adventure. Migrants were required to stay for two years, giving up their passports on arrival, able only to return to Britain if they paid back their outward fare in full, in addition to paying for their journey home. At the beginning of the period there was a focus on assisting migrants who had certain skill sets such as building tradesmen or nurses, but by the 1960s there was less emphasis placed on these requirements. A preference for married migrants under the age of 51 and for single migrants under 46 remained. Health checks were conducted to ensure applicants suffering from diseases such as tuberculosis were not accepted. Other overseas opportunities for women included working as an au pair, a governess or in teaching and academia. For men, there were roles in management in former colonies. One such role was to be found in the rubber plantations of Malaysia which gained independence from Britain in 1957.

Life on a Rubber Plantation: After an interview and upon acceptance, young men would sign up for anywhere between 4 and 7 years. The initial role was as trainee estate manager. Even though it afforded great privilege, it was not without hardship. For many it was their first time away from home comforts and family. They would have to learn how to tap rubber (though this would never be their job), speak Malay and get used to the sweltering heat which necessitated starting work at sunrise. Anyone who couldn't hack it would not only have to fund their own fare home, but in many cases would have to pay the company for their outward journey. This could lead to great financial hardship. If the trainee gained promotion to estate manager, they were afforded a driver and a housekeeper. Although they were masters of all they surveyed, they faced a difficult balancing act. Local Malays were employed as clearers of the jungle with Tamils (originally from Southern India) and Chinese employed as rubber tappers. Keeping everybody happy was a difficult juggling act, compounded by the fact that there was a Chinese communist led insurgency. There were shops on the estate where products from home could be bought at great expense. The savvy Brit soon learned to eat as locals did at a fraction of the cost. After work, there was always the club where ex-pats could mingle. Gin in the afternoon, whisky in the evening and settle the bill at the end of the month, was the general rule.

Women's Work

With the exception of the two World Wars when women filled jobs otherwise undertaken by men who were posted overseas, the role of women was little changed for decades. In the early 1960s things were about to change, but only very slowly. In 1962/3 only one quarter of university students studying in Great Britain were women. Even upon graduation things were still unequal. It was only in 1961 that legislation was passed giving women equal pay in the civil service. It wasn't until 1975 that it became illegal to sack a woman for being pregnant. Women could legally be refused service to spend their own money in a pub. This law didn't change until 1982. Women who had gained equal suffrage with men in 1928 increasingly

Women mostly occupied administrative roles

began to demand a right to a proper education, equal pay and affordable childcare. But for most women their work would be in the home. It would start with making breakfast for the whole family, then making sure that the husband was suitably attired for work and that the children were ready for school. Next it was onto the chores: dusting, cleaning, washing, making beds and ironing. Since most houses still didn't have fridges, shopping was a daily task. As supermarkets were a rarity, this required visits to several shops: the butcher, the baker, the greengrocer and mainly on Fridays the fishmonger. The only thing that was delivered to the house in those days was milk. If she found time in the middle of the day, the 60s housewife might have a nice cup of tea with a neighbour. It was then time to collect the children from school and feed them. After that, she would prepare a supper for her husband, which they would eat together. Then it would be time to put the children to bed, reminding them to brush their teeth

The daily chores of a 1960s housewife

and wash their faces. Although it was a man's world, most fathers saw little of their children except at weekends. Women did gain employment but, with some exceptions, this was mainly outside the demands of childcare. Schools reflected this. Girls would learn what were known then as domestic sciences: cooking, sewing and household management. After leaving school, some women trained for secretarial roles; the role of school secretary being highly prized as it allowed holidays to coincide with their children's. The 1960s were a time of rapid social and economic change and by the end of the decade attitudes had changed, even though legislation trailed behind.

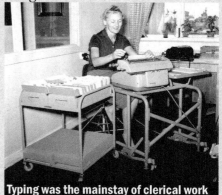
Typing was the mainstay of clerical work

Farming

A typical post-war tractor with open cab

IR8 seeds being packed (credit: IRRI)

Whisky maturing in white oak casks

Although the farm of the 1960s looked very different from the farm of today, increased mechanisation meant that they also looked markedly different from the pre-war farm. Fields were smaller and more work had to be done by hand than today. However, by the end of the decade the greater reliance on machinery not only shaped the crops that were grown (potatoes in particular leant themselves to machine sowing and harvesting), it also saw a 40% decline in the number of farmworkers. Even though the government had brought in controls on pesticides a decade earlier, there was a heavy reliance on chemicals both as pesticides and fertilisers. This was to have serious health implications, not only for farmworkers, but also for the general population. Farms were also dangerous places to work. The tractor, as well as being the most iconic piece of farm machinery, was also the most deadly. An annual average of 43 people were killed from 1957 to 1967 as a result of tractors overturning. This represented over one-third of work-related fatalities in agriculture. It was not until 1967 that legislation was introduced requiring all new tractors to be fitted with safety cabs.

In the 1960s new strains of fruit and vegetables were being developed. The most significant advance came half-way around the world in India. The country was facing impending rice shortages which would inevitably lead to famine. In 1963, Peter Jennings and Henry Beachell, two American plant breeders, were one year into a project where they successfully cross-bred high yield rice from Indonesia with a dwarf rice from China. The result became known as IR8; by the end of the decade yields soared and millions of lives were saved. In Scotland a similar, though not as spectacular, thing was happening with the production of new strains of barley at the expense of oats and turnips. Although barley has many uses, such as making malted drinks and adding to soups, it was chiefly grown for the Whisky industry.* Fuelled by rising demand from overseas markets such as America and Japan, the 1960s were boom years for Scottish distillers.

*There has been much debate between whisky connoisseurs, with many claiming that scotch was a much better drink before the 1960s. While this is of course a matter of personal taste, there is no doubt that the rapid expansion of the industry and the way whisky was produced changed the tipple forever. As well as switching to high yield barley, distilling techniques changed as did the way the final product was stored. Previously, Spanish sherry casks were used, but by the 1960s these had been replaced by American ex-bourbon white oak casks. This made the final product smoother and more attractive to the American palate. The industry has grown to become Britain's largest food and drink export. This multi-billion pound industry brings in 5 times the revenue of the second biggest, namely chocolate.

The Primary School

In the 1960s there were no state pre-schools or nurseries, so for most children just turning 5 years old, their first day at school was the first time they had been on their own away from home. Many mothers did not work outside the home, so this was also the first time they had been away from the home environment. Consequently, the first day of school was often a very tearful event for both child and parent. Having got over the first pangs of separation, school life soon fell into a predictable routine of learning the times tables, handwriting skills and reading out loud. School milk was part of this routine, and in the summer months it could

An older class busy painting pictures

easily turn sour. In post-war Britain, a third of a pint of milk per child, was introduced in schools to supplement the child's diet. In 1971, school milk for the over-sevens was withdrawn by Margaret Thatcher, then Secretary of State for Education. For this she was dubbed 'Thatcher, Thatcher, Milk Snatcher' in the popular press. During the harsh winter of 1962-3, or the big freeze of 1963 as it became known, it was a common sight to see the small crates of milk outside the school gates with the shiny bottle tops standing proud above the bottles on a column of frozen milk. Of course the only way to defrost the school milk was to place it by the radiator, and then the poor children were forced to consume watery, lukewarm milk. And forced they were: "milk is good for your child, you WILL drink it all up!" The School Broadcasting Council for the United Kingdom had been set up in 1947 and the wireless or radio played a great part

Harvest festival celebrations

in the education of school children in the 1960s. *Music and Movement* was one such programme. All over the country in school halls, children could be found leaping and stretching to the commands on the radio. 'Now children we are going to sway like trees in the wind' would be the instruction on the radio, so all the children would begin to sway with their arms in the air. There was no 'gym kit' in primary schools so the children just removed their outer clothes and did physical education in their vests, knickers or underpants and bare feet or pumps (usually purchased from F.W. Woolworth). Visits from the school nurse would break up the daily routine. The nit nurse used to make regular visits to check for head lice.

All the children in each class would line up to be examined in turn, their hair being combed carefully with a nit comb to see if there was any infestation. There were also routine eye and hearing tests, and visits from the school dentist. Class sizes in the early 1960s were large, often over 30 children to a class, as these were the 'baby boomers', children born after the Second World War. There were no classroom assistants, just the class teacher and discipline was strict. It was quite common for a disruptive child to be rapped over the knuckles, on the buttocks or on the palm of the hand with a ruler.

A Christmas party at a school in Wales

Background

After the Second World War, the state funded secondary education system was divided using a Tripartite system containing grammar schools, secondary technical colleges and secondary modern schools. The Eleven-plus examination was used to select which pupils went to which schools based on ability. As technical colleges were not available on the scale envisaged the exam came to symbolise fierce competition for places at the prestigious grammar schools. The very name still deeply divides opinion with many believing it was the symbol of a segregated two-tier school system whilst for others it set the educational benchmark.

Here's your chance to test yourself with example questions from the 1960s:
(Answers on page 94)

Arithmetic Questions

Question One: A train leaves London at 10:30am and arrives at Birmingham at 12:40pm. It stopped from 12:10pm to 12:20pm at Coventry which is 100 miles from London. It travelled both parts of the journey at the same rate. Find the distance from London to Birmingham.

Question Two: If 1st December falls on a Monday, on what day will Christmas Day fall that year?

Question Three: A machine makes toy soldiers at the rate of 75 in 5 minutes. How long with it take to make 6,000 of them? (answer in hours and minutes)

Question Four: Write in figures the sum of four hundred and forty six and seventy-seven.

Question Five: John is 12 years old and his mother is 42. Answer the following:

A) How old was John's mother when she was 4 times as old as him?

B) In how many years' time will his mother be three times as old as John?

C) How old will John be when his mother is 10 times as old as he was 6 years ago?

General English Questions

Question One: Change all necessary words to make these sentences plural:

A) My dog is carrying a stick.
B) His butcher has no meat.
C) A man who likes football is sure to have a team scarf in his house.

Question Two: Fill in the blank with a suitable missing word:

A) As *toe* is to *foot* so is .... to *hand*.
B) As *referee* is to *football* so is .... to *tennis*
C) As *Spain* is to .... so is *France* to *Frenchmen*

Question Three: Rewrite each of these sentences replacing the underlined words with a single word:

A) I was <u>in no doubt</u> that the shop would be closed.
B) He said that he would be coming home <u>in a short time</u>.
C) She <u>made up her mind</u> to go the cinema.

Top 10 Girls' Baby Names [1]

1. Susan — of Hebrew origin meaning "Lily Rose"
2. Julie — of French/Latin origin meaning "Youthful"
3. Karen — of Danish origin possibly via Ancient Greek Katharos meaning "Pure"
4. Jaqueline — from Hebrew via French meaning "may God protect"
5. Deborah — derived from the Hebrew word D'vorah meaning "Bee"
6. Tracey — from French and Gaelic Irish meaning "higher" or "superior"
7. Jane — from the Hebrew meaning "God is Merciful"
8. Helen — possibly from the Greek Selene meaning "Moon"
9. Diane — from Latin via French meaning "Divine"
10. Sharon — from Hebrew meaning "of the fertile plain"

Top 10 Boys' Baby Names [2]

1. David — corruption of the Hebrew name *Dawid* meaning "beloved"
2. Paul — from Latin meaning "Small" or "Humble"
3. Andrew — of Greek origin meaning "Garland or crown"
4. Mark — from the Latin name Mart-kos "consecrated to the god Mars"
5. John — of Hebrew origin meaning "God is Gracious"
6. Michael — of Hebrew origin meaning "One who is like God"
7. Stephen — of origin meaning "garland or crown"
8. Ian — a variation of John meaning "God is Gracious"
9. Robert — from the Old German meaning "Fame Bright"
10. Richard — from Old German meaning "Powerful leader"

[1] [2] Data compiled by the Office for National Statistics 1964

Games, Toys and Pastimes

In 1963 the toy of the year in Britain was Mousetrap, a multi-player game which was one of the first mass-produced three-dimensional board games. In it the players must first cooperate to build a mousetrap from plastic pieces, then all hell breaks loose in the second part of the game when participants attempt to trap their opponents' mice. The Chatter Telephone by Fisher-Price was also popular. It first came on the market in 1962 and was a pull along toy which worked like a dial-up telephone. Right through to the 1970s it was the company's best selling toy. In these simpler times there was also a plethora of kitchen toys such as the easy-bake oven, which taught mostly girls domestic science. Most children noticed that the moulded plastic pies and cakes looked the same after they came out of the oven as before they went in, so little was learnt. Card and board games were popular, seeing families gather and perhaps fall out over a game of Monopoly, Cluedo or Happy Families. The first computer game, Spacewar!, was developed at the Massachusetts Institute of Technology. Its graphics were basic and the unit it ran on was the size of a car. Children would have to wait until 1977 for something more sophisticated when Atari produced Pong, a simple game based on table tennis.

Relaxing in the front room, this family has chosen some of the design trends that would come to define home furnishing in the 1960s. Despite the black and white photo it is clear to see the bold patterns on the sitting room chairs. The clashing patterns and vivid colours that would dominate the latter half of the 1960s were already evident in 1963 as consumers with increasing disposable income aspired to make over their austere post-war home interiors.

The trend for clean lines and functional design was most obvious in the kitchen with the rise of fitted cabinetry and integrated appliances.

Record players were the mainstay of entertainment in most households. Here we see a father about to play an EP (extended play) record for his boys. EP's were a popular format in the UK until the late sixties.

With television programming for children limited to the odd programme per day, children would still spend most of their indoor time reading, drawing and playing games sat either at the dining table or on the floor in the lounge.

In the bathroom, homeowners were keen to modernise and update the layout to include fitted baths, vanity sink units and close coupled toilets. The picture above shows a lady cleaning the bath with an integrated shower attachment.

Children lucky enough to live in houses with a good sized garden would spend hours playing outdoors building dens, creating adventures and enjoying picnics. However, the park and the street were just as popular.

Design Trends in the Early Sixties

With increasing living standards and demand for modern home interiors the 1960s were a fertile time for design. British designers were making waves on the global stage as manufacturers invested in product development and aesthetic design. New materials and manufacturing techniques gave greater freedom to innovate. The trend saw sleek and streamlined furniture designs being complimented by patterned fabric textures and wall papers. With sustained economic growth during this period, British consumer confidence grew significantly as the public finally laid to rest the period of post-war shortages and austerity. This confidence was most obviously expressed in the increasing use of vivid colours in the home whether that be the carpets, the furniture or the wall coverings. Consumerism was most definitely on the rise. In the fifties, ownership of home appliances such as fridges or televisions was the preserve of the privileged few but by the early sixties it became the norm.

Whilst British design was gaining favour globally, the most influential design trends were emanating from the USA, Italy and Scandinavia. The Mid-Century Modern design movement in the USA was popular from 1945 to 1969. Its hallmarks were clean, simple lines and honest use of materials. Similar in ethos was the Scandinavian design movement which started to flourish in the 1950s. At its heart were the principles of simplicity, minimalism and functionality. Although the United Kingdom would have to wait until 1987 before seeing its first store open, the behemoth that is IKEA, founded by Ingvar Kamprad, was growing and developing in Sweden in 1962 and soon to expand to nearby Norway in 1963.

When in 1960 Elizabeth David produced her greatest work *French Provincial Cooking*, the Observer newspaper noted: "It is difficult to think that any home can do without it." By 1963, it had found its way onto the bookshelves of many homes around the country. By following her recipes British home cooks had embraced flavour and rescued culinary tastes from the bland Victorian fare prescribed by Mrs Beeton, whose recipes included an instruction to cook pasta for one and a half hours. David's path to domestic goddess status was an unorthodox one. She was born into an upper class family and came out as a debutante in 1932, but none of the men she met at various balls appealed to her. She then tried her hand at art and acting, both without much enthusiasm. It was while appearing with fellow actress Anna Neagle, that Neagle noted the young David did not even know how to make a cup of

tea. When David's family suspected her of having an affair with a married man, they packed her off to the continent. It was there that she not only embraced the culture, but immersed herself in the cuisine. The resultant cookery books and humorous journals would change British tastes forever.

A Classic Gratin Dauphinois Recipe (Serves 6)

Ingredients

- 2 lbs Desiree Potatoes (which had been bred in the Netherlands in 1962. However, King Edwards will do)
- 10 fl oz full fat milk
- 10 fl oz double cream
- 2 oz butter
- 1 garlic clove, peeled and halved
- 2 sprigs of fresh thyme, plus extra for sprinkling
- 1 shallot, roughly chopped (although a small onion would do)
- A pinch of finely grated nutmeg
- 1 oz freshly grated parmesan (a hard British cheese could also be used)
- Salt and pepper to taste

Method: Preheat the oven to Gas mark 4/ 160 degrees. Rub the butter all over the inside of a large shallow dish (about 18 by 11 inches). Peel and thinly slice the potatoes (approx 1/8" thick). Lay the slices on a tea towel and pat them dry. Keep them covered while preparing the rest of the ingredients. Pour the milk and cream into a saucepan. Add the garlic, thyme and shallot. Slowly warm the milk until just before it boils and then remove from the heat. Strain the liquid into a large jug and sprinkle with nutmeg. Layer about half the potatoes in the dish and season. Pour over half the milk and cream. Repeat with the remaining ingredients. Scatter the cheese over the top and bake for around an hour, when the potatoes should be tender and the topping golden brown. Leave to stand for 5 minutes and sprinkle over the remaining thyme. Bon appetit.

In the early 1960s pudding made up a substantial part of most meals, be it at school or in the home. Some were fulsomely enjoyed and have stayed firm favourites, whilst others have not. Although the food producer Ambrosia had resumed production of both tinned rice and tinned macaroni puddings after the war, it was more common for them to be home-made. Other favourite puddings included jam roly-poly, chocolate sponge with chocolate sauce, apple crumble, bread and butter pudding and blancmange. Acquired tastes included sago and tapioca puddings. There was also the pudding that made schoolboys giggle, Spotted Dick, which was also known as spotted dog or railway cake, which avoided double entendres.

Spotted Dick Recipe   (Serves 8)

Ingredients

- 10 oz self-raising flour
- 5 oz shredded suet
- 6 oz currants
- 4 oz caster sugar
- 2 oz mixed dried peel
- ¼ pint of milk, plus 3 tablespoons
- A pinch of salt

Method: Put the flour and salt into a mixing bowl. Add the suet, currants, sugar and mixed peel. Pour in the milk and mix to a firm but moist dough, adding extra milk if necessary. Shape into a fat roll about 8 inches long and wrap loosely in baking parchment, tying both ends with string, This will allow the pudding to rise. Place a steamer over a large pan of boiling water, add the wrapped pudding to the steamer and cook for 1½ hours. Check periodically whether the saucepan has run dry. Top up with water if necessary. Remove the pudding from the steamer and allow to cool slightly before unwrapping. Serve with custard.

Summer Holidays in 1963

In 1963 there were more choices on where to spend your hard-earned cash on a once-a-year holiday than ever before. At the top end was the growing cruise ship market. Choices included the recently launched SS Canberra. At 45,000 tons it was the largest vessel to pass through the Panama Canal to date. Competing at the luxury end of the market was the SS France, replete with two on-board swimming pools. European sun-soaked holidays were beginning to take off. In 1957 British European

The SS Canberra was an ocean liner in the P&O fleet

The swimming pool at Butlin's Pwllheli

Airways (BEA) had introduced a route to Alicante in Eastern Spain. The term Costa Blanca was created to promote it. However, a ferry was still a more affordable way to travel with popular destinations including France, Belgium, Holland and Ireland. However, most people still holidayed at home. There were many options: the holiday camps (Warner, Butlin's or Pontins), an independently run caravan park, a bed and breakfast by the sea or simply staying with a relative by the coast. For some people all the fun of the fair came to them, be it in the form of the Highland Games in Scotland, the Grasmere Games in the Lake District or the Eisteddfod in Wales. Another popular event that draws travellers from all over the UK and beyond is the Edinburgh Fringe Festival. Starting as an unofficial adjunct to the Edinburgh International Festival in 1947, the name 'Fringe' was first coined a year later. By 1963 the Fringe was firmly established in the August calendar. In this year, the artistic credentials of the festival were cemented with the establishment of the Traverse Theatre which would present cutting edge dramas.

Enjoying the Eisteddfod festival in Wales

A family camping trip was a popular summer holiday choice

Radio Butlin was an integral part of the Butlin's camp experience, as immortalised in the TV sitcom Hi-De-Hi.

Campers were assigned into 'Houses' for all the sports, games and competitions. Rivalry was friendly but intense!

The Ladies Dancing competition was judged with points for the winner going towards their House total.

The inter-house Tug of War competition was particularly competitive. It drew big crowds cheering the teams on.

Children's entertainer, Uncle Boko, is pictured here presenting the "Father and Son" competition.

Redcoats would be assigned to tables to eat with campers to continue the Butlin's experience through mealtimes.

The houndstooth coat was a popular fashion item in 1963. The tessellated pattern of broken checks was most commonly black and white but other colour combinations were available, including dark red/white.

Riding a Vespa scooter, this model is wearing a light-coloured polo neck jumper with tartan waistcoat over and matching capri pants.

At a youth fashion show, the model is wearing a polo neck and checkered trousers. Note the fashionable hairstyles in the room!

This yoke-top shift dress, complete with matching jacket, has a naval feel.

Christmas 1963

In some ways the Christmases of the early 1960's were very similar to that of today. Families gathered together and shared much laughter and fun. But whereas today the celebrations often centre around lavish presents and the use of social media, then the celebrations were more home-made. Greeting cards would be sent to all members of the family, often the only written communication of the year. Some would contain news of the past year including news of how well the children were doing at school or in sports. In 1963 the telephone bore a greater resemblance to a table lamp than the devices of today. Calls were brief with salutations and felicitations being exchanged, all the time keeping an eye on the cost. The days of post-war rationing were still all too recent memories, so Christmas had a more frugal feel compared to today. Decorations were simple and improvised.

Tucking in to Christmas treats

Brightly coloured paper chains were made by the family and strung across the walls in the living room. If money was tight, these could be made from strips of wallpaper. Children's TV programme Blue Peter was at hand to show you how to make your own decorations. Many of these defied health and safety standards, including how to make an advent crown from wire coat hangers, with a lit candle at each end! Food preparation began weeks, if not months, in advance. The fruit for the pudding would be steeped in alcohol, and when ready would be stirred into the batter along with a silver sixpence for luck. Few people had home freezers, so all the components of the Christmas lunch had to be purchased as close

Visiting Santa at his grotto

as possible to the big day. Members of the family were sent out to all four corners of the town or village to collect orders from the butcher, greengrocer and the baker as supermarkets were in their infancy. On Christmas Eve, parents would prepare a feast of mince pies and sherry (whisky in Scotland) for Father Christmas, which would disappear by morning. Sometimes a carrot would also be left for Rudolph. Children left stockings or pillow cases by their beds ready to be filled with gifts, but only if they had been good, of course! Main presents were opened after breakfast: for children these might be a watch (perhaps a Tic-a-Tic-a-Timex), Scalextric or a Sindy doll. Other favourite gifts included Etch-a-Sketch, Meccano, 3D View Master and the Amazing Magic Robot that answered questions. Relatives might also bring home made gifts, such as hand knitted jumpers and scarves. As there were no shops open on Christmas Day, the words "batteries not included" led to an occasional tearful afternoon as shops would not reopen until after Boxing Day. The day itself was one of indulgence. Very often a full English breakfast was served in the morning. The dinner itself was not always turkey as, often, the meat of choice might be chicken or goose. The best tablecloth, china, glasses and silverware were brought out for this most special of occasions, before being packed away for another year.

A festive family portrait around the tree

The most notable development of 1963 was the rise to fame of The Beatles. Their first album, *Please Please Me*, was released in March 1963 and marked the beginning of a run during which eleven of their twelve studio albums released in the United Kingdom up to 1970 reached number one. The third single, *From Me To You* came out in April, starting an almost unbroken string of seventeen British number one singles for the band. Their impact on American television and radio audiences in November 1963 also marked the beginning of the so-called *British Invasion* of the US charts by British bands. The year also

The Beatles in 1963

saw the founding of The Kinks, led by the brothers Ray and Dave Davies. In America, The March On Washington on 28th August is best remembered for Martin Luther King Jr.'s "I Have

Frank Sinatra

a Dream" speech, but it also featured singers from the protest movement such as Mahalia Jackson, Joan Baez and Bob Dylan. In classical music, Benjamin Britten not only celebrated his fiftieth birthday, but also produced a recording of his most celebrated work, *War Requiem*. It sold 200,000 copies, which was almost unheard of for a classical work. It would probably have sold more had the record label, Decca, anticipated the demand on both sides of the Atlantic. The work deservedly won 3 Grammy Awards. On 8th April, the 35th Academy Awards ceremony took place at the Santa Monica Civic Auditorium. It was hosted by "Ol' Blue Eyes" himself, Frank Sinatra. It honoured the best films of 1962 with *Lawrence of Arabia* winning best picture and David Lean being awarded Best Director, making it a good day for British cinema. Back at home, things were different. Cinema attendances, which hit a peak of 1.63 billion admissions in 1946 had declined by over three-quarters to 357 million by 1963. It was

a trend that would continue for the rest of the decade as the allure and the comfort of watching television at home replaced the attraction of the big screen. 1963 was a pivotal moment in British theatre with the founding of the National Theatre in London, under the directorship of the nation's greatest thespian, Laurence Olivier. Between 1963 and 1976 the company was based at the Old Vic in Waterloo. The first performance in October was a widely acclaimed production of *Hamlet*, with Peter O'Toole in the title role. *Alfie*, which most people know as a 1966 film starring Michael Caine and a 2004 re-make starring Jude Law, began its life as a radio play in 1962. It was reworked for the stage by Bill Naughton and ran at London's Mermaid Theatre from 19th June to 13th July 1963. It later transferred to Broadway with Terrence Stamp playing the part of Alfie. Radio was still a big part of people's lives in Britain. However, there was very little that was

Laurence Olivier

aimed at the youth market provided by, the then monopoly broadcaster, the BBC. *The Light Programme* (never a title to appeal to the young) did have *Pick of the Pops*, presented by Alan "Fluff" Freeman. His welcoming cry of "Greetings, pop pickers" each Sunday sent listeners seeking more exciting fare by tuning in to alternative and more edgy stations such as Radio Luxembourg and Radio Hilversum.

Billy Liar

Actor Tom Courtenay

Starring Tom Courtenay and Julie Christie
Directed by John Schlesinger
Released: 16th September 1963 (UK)

Featuring an extraordinary acting performance by Tom Courtenay, *Billy Liar* starts off as a farce. Courtenay's Billy lives in a fantasy world, or a fantasy country, where he is the dictator, passing back and forth between a Churchill-like autocrat who inspires his people with magnificent Churchillian speeches to a Hitler-esque fascist. The fantasies are played out in real flesh and blood for us, and they are quite striking, and occasionally hilariously absurd. An imaginary series of regiments parades before Billy, including one in which all the members have lost their right arms. Billy imagines himself leading each regiment, including a corps from India, make-up included. He also repeatedly turns on his perceived real-life enemies with a fantasy machine gun. He gets a job in a funeral home of all places, but never seems to do any work. The genius of the movie, however, is that Billy grows more complex as the film moves along. He has somehow got himself engaged to two different girls, neither of whom he intends to marry, and bizarrely keeps running into both of them. As he increasingly gets more caught in his own various webs of deceit, Billy begins to crack, and as the audience see how emotionally vulnerable he really is, he becomes much more a figure to pity. Courtenay is masterful, as he seeks to keep hold of his fantasies and juggle his many lies, without getting trapped and caught; it doesn't always work.

The Birds

Starring Rod Taylor, Jessica Tandy and Tippi Hedren
Directed by Alfred Hitchcock
Released: 29th March 1963 (US)

The film is a psychological horror-thriller based on a short story by Daphne du Maurier. The story follows a wealthy socialite named Melanie Daniels, played by Tippi Hedren, who travels to the small town of Bodega Bay in California to pursue a man she's interested in. Upon her arrival, she is attacked by a seagull. This is only the beginning of a series of bizarre and terrifying bird attacks that take over the town. As the attacks become more frequent and violent, the townspeople struggle to understand the reason behind the birds' sudden aggression. Melanie and a local schoolteacher, played by Rod Taylor, attempt to survive and uncover the cause of the bird attacks. Hitchcock masterfully builds tension throughout the film with eerie sound effects, haunting imagery and a lack of background music, making it all the more unnerving. The film's climax takes place in a suspenseful and chaotic scene at a farmhouse, where the main characters face an onslaught of attacking birds. *The Birds* is considered a classic in the horror-thriller genre and is praised for its innovative use of special effects and suspenseful storytelling. Its ambiguous ending leaves the audience with a sense of unease and also uncertainty about what could have caused the birds to attack.

Charade

Starring Audrey Hepburn, Cary Grant and Walter Matthau
Directed by Stanley Donen
Released: 5th December 1963 (US)

The story follows Regina Lampert (Hepburn), a young woman who returns to Paris from a skiing holiday to find that her husband has been murdered and all their assets have disappeared. She soon learns that her husband was involved in the theft of a large sum of money during World War II. Several men are now after the money, believing that Regina knows its whereabouts. One of these men is Peter Joshua (Grant), a charming stranger who helps Regina navigate her way through the dangerous world of espionage and betrayal. As they work together to solve the mystery, Regina and Peter's relationship deepens, and they fall in love. The film's screenplay, written by Peter Stone, is noted for its clever plot twists and witty dialogue. The chemistry between Hepburn and Grant is also a highlight, as they bring their trademark charm and sophistication to their roles. *Charade* was a critical and commercial success upon its release and has since become a beloved classic. Its iconic score, composed by Henry Mancini, features the hit song *Charade*, which was nominated for an Academy Award for Best Original Song. Due to the suspense, the presence of Cary Grant, the structure of the screenplay and the frequent plot twists, many people believed this was a Hitchcock film. This confusion has prompted fans of the film to call it "the best Hitchcock film Hitchcock never made."

Hud

Starring Paul Newman, Brandon deWilde, Melvyn Douglas, Patricia Neal
Directed by Martin Ritt
Released: 30th May 1963 (UK)

On a Texas cattle ranch, young buck Lonnie Brannon (deWilde) finds himself torn between two family figures: his righteous and inflexibly traditional grandfather, Homer (Douglas) and his immoral, self-serving uncle, Hud (Newman). The film is an adaptation of Larry McMurtry's novel *Horseman, Pass By* and is as much a "King Lear"-esque patriarchal melodrama as it is a parable of moral decay and capitalist irresponsibility in the stark but sincere dressings of a revisionist Western. James Wong Howe's filtered black & white photography of the desolate landscapes is memorable, as are the performances.

Douglas and Neal both won Oscars, the latter inexplicably for a lead performance, even though she's only on-screen for about twenty minutes. It's Newman who's the real standout, playing a remarkably arrogant and unsympathetic character, yet the actor's irrepressible magnetism makes him an anti-hero instead of an antagonist. Indistinct motivations and a leisurely pace at the outset contribute to its slow burner feel. The lead-up to the resolution has enough painterly contrivances to see every brushstroke, but the acting and timeless family drama bedrock overcomes the deficits.

Jason and the Argonauts

Starring Todd Armstrong, Honor Blackman and Douglas Wilmer
Directed by Don Chaffey
Released: 15th August 1963 (UK)

The film begins with a power-hungry warrior named Pelias (Wilmer) who decides to seize the throne of the King of Iolos. However, once that is accomplished, he is told of a prophecy that one of the King's children will eventually take it from him. So he decides to kill all of the King's children as well. Unfortunately, in the process of trying to do that he deliberately profanes the temple of Hera (Blackman), who then angrily allows the King's infant son Jason (Armstrong) to be carried away to safety. She warns Pelias to beware of a one-sandaled man. Twenty years later, Jason saves Pelias from drowning but loses a sandal in the process. Recognising his enemy, Pelias urges Jason to set sail in search of a legendary golden fleece belonging to the gods. Fraught with danger, Pelias hopes that Jason will perish on his quest. Jason assembles a crew and sets sail on the Argo in search of the fleece. During an epic voyage he battles harpies, a giant bronze Talos and a skeleton army.

The special effects by Ray Harryhausen were years, if not decades, ahead of their time. In fact, the effects were too much for the British censors at the time and a brief scene was cut from a skeleton fight where the decapitated skeleton is seen feeling around for its head.

Sid Caesar (left) and
Jonathan Winters (right)

It's a Mad, Mad, Mad, Mad World

Starring Spencer Tracy, Milton Berle, Ethel Merman and Sid Caesar
Directed by Stanley Kramer
Released: 3rd December 1963 (UK)

The film follows the story of a group of strangers who, after witnessing a car accident, embark on a frantic race to find buried treasure. The plot begins with a dying man revealing to a group of strangers the location of $350,000 in stolen money buried under a "big W" in a nearby park. The group then sets out on a wild goose chase to find the money, encountering numerous obstacles and comical mishaps along the way. As the search for the treasure intensifies, the group divides into several factions, each trying to outsmart and outwit the others. The film's climax takes place at the Santa Rosita Airport, where the characters engage in a madcap chase involving planes, helicopters and a fire engine. Despite its lengthy runtime of nearly three hours, *It's a Mad, Mad, Mad, Mad World* remains a beloved classic of American cinema, known for its fast-paced humour, slapstick comedy and memorable performances. The film's all-star cast and elaborate stunt work also contribute to its enduring popularity. While the film was not initially a critical success, it has since gained a cult following and is widely regarded as one of the greatest comedy films of all time. Its influence can be seen in countless other comedies, and its legacy continues to inspire filmmakers and audiences today.

Doctor Who

Starring William Hartnell as "The Doctor"
First aired 23ʳᵈ November 1963

The TARDIS

Doctor Who had the most inauspicious of starts. It first aired a day after the assassination of US President JFK. In addition, there were several power cuts across the UK on that day. But like The Doctor himself, it endured, becoming one of the most successful British TV programmes of all time. In the very first episode, school teachers Barbara Wright (Jacqueline Hill) and Ian Chesterton (William Russell) are concerned about a strange student named Susan Foreman (Carole Ann Ford), who seems to have extraordinary insight on many subjects, and yet is strangely ignorant on everyday things such as money. She's also very vague about where she lives, so the two teachers decide to secretly follow her home one evening. They're led to what looks like a police call box in the middle of a junkyard. They then meet Susan's grandfather, a mysterious, cantankerous figure known only as The Doctor (William Hartnell). Susan reveals that she and the Doctor are aliens from another planet and from another time, and that the call-box is actually a ship called the TARDIS (Time And Relative Dimension(s) In Space) capable of travelling through time and space. To prove it, they go back in time to the year 100,000 B. C., where they end up battling against hostile cave people who are trying to learn the secret of fire. It wasn't long before fans saw the debut of *Doctor Who's* most famous enemy the Dalek. They were first seen in a seven-parter which was first screened on 21ˢᵗ December 1963.

The Dick Emery Show

Starring Dick Emery, Pat Coombs, Deryck Guyler, Roy Kinnear, Joan Sims
Ran from 13ᵗʰ July 1963 to 7ᵗʰ February 1981

Dick Emery

The BBC1 show was a fixture of Saturday night television for the best part of two decades. Emery was not strictly speaking an impressionist; rather than copy famous people, he had his own repertoire of outrageous comic characters. Among them was the buck-toothed 'The Reverend Chislet', a bespectacled spinster called 'Hettie' whose determination to get a man knew no bounds and the lovable old codger 'James Maynard Kitchener Lampwick'. There was also 'Gaylord Screwsby', the bovver boy (often accompanied by his similarly attired father, played by Roy Kinnear, who would try without success to give his son a masterclass in crime). Others included the upper-class tramp 'College', camp-as-a-row-of-tents 'Clarence', and not forgetting sex-pot 'Mandy' (whose favourite saying was 'ooh you are awful, but I like you!'). Each week, these characters inhabited sketches usually written by John Warren and John Singer, beginning with a vox pop scene on film, in which a typically B.B.C. interviewer, Gordon Clyde, stopped passers-by to ask questions. Encountering Mandy, he invariably wound up being pushed backwards into a hedge. In many ways it was a precursor to other character-driven sketch shows like *The Fast Show*, but viewed through today's eyes it seems dated and out-of-touch. It may have been "of its time", but it still was innovative and had many genuinely funny moments. The show featured writers Marty Feldman, Barry Cryer and future Nobel Laureate Harold Pinter.

The Des O'Connor Show

Produced by Associated Television (ATV)
Ran from 29th May 1963 to 28th December 1973

Des O'Connor

By 1963 Des O'Connor was a successful singer, but his fame was about to rocket as he was given his own chat show. He was a jack-of-all-trades in the entertainment world who, having started out as a Redcoat at Butlin's holiday camps, used the skills he honed there as a singer, stand-up comedian, chat-show host, game-show compère and cabaret and musical theatre performer. Not for nothing was he often described as the "ultimate entertainer". His supposed deficiencies as a performer became the basis for a long-standing joke on Morecambe and Wise's television programmes. O'Connor was always happy to send himself up and he even contributed quite a few of the insults to the pair's repertoire. It was easy to underestimate quite how successful a career he enjoyed. By any standard, O'Connor was enormously popular, and operated at the pinnacle of the light entertainment world. His nearest rivals for longevity at the top of the forms in which he worked were probably Bruce Forsyth and Cliff Richard. *The Des O'Connor Show* ran for 8 series until 1973 and was latterly syndicated to more than 40 countries, including the NBC network in America. It was succeeded, in 1977 by *Des O'Connor Tonight* which ran for 7 series on the BBC and then a further 17 on ITV; it last aired in 2002. Throughout the 1960s seasons he welcomed guests such as Lulu, Tom Jones and Barbara Windsor, who all provided a mixture of cabaret and mirth.

That Was The Week That Was

Presenter: David Frost

Cast: Millicent Martin; Kenneth Cope; Roy Kinnear; Bernard Levin et al.

TW3 Opening Titles

That Was the Week That Was, which quickly became known as *TW3*, was a daring satirical look at current affairs featuring sketches, humorous songs and parodies of the news. However, the programme that was the first to bring satire to British televisions almost didn't appear at all. The BBC commissioned a pilot of the show but had concerns about lampooning their political masters. After all, it was in the power of politicians to renew or end the BBC's licence. Word spread that the newly created ITV (commercial television) were about to poach Frost and steal the show's format, so *TW3* was quickly given the green light by the BBC. Frost presented as if born to the format with the show becoming an instant success. The studio set up was enormously influential for future television with previously hidden scaffolding and cameras clearly on show, all of which added to the edginess of *TW3*. The show also gained from being in the right place at the right time. Prime Minister Harold Macmillan, who had previously been portrayed as "SuperMac", was beginning to see his world crumble around him. A disastrous Cabinet reshuffle, dubbed the "Night of the Long Knives" and the later sex scandal, the Profumo affair, gave the team much to work with. Macmillan was apparently laid back about *TW3*. However, in 1963, the BBC's cold feet resurfaced and they pulled the show. In its short life, *That Was the Week That Was* had changed the landscape of TV forever.

Phil Silvers and the cast

The New Phil Silvers Show

Starring Phil Silvers, Stafford Repp, Herbie Faye and Elena Verdugo
First aired 28th September 1963

Phil Silvers' career spanned more than 60 years. He was best known for his portrayal of Sergeant Bilko in the 1950s series *You'll Never Get Rich*, which later became *The Phil Silvers Show*. The sitcom was set in a motor pool on an army base and saw the title character Sgt. Bilko, gambling, conniving and cheating all in a bid to get-rich-quick. The show was an enormous success, often repeated around the world. In 1963, Silvers reprised the role, this time in civvy street. In the new series he played Harry Grafton, a factory foreman, who guess what? was a gambling, conniving cheat interested in get-rich-quick schemes. One worked, the other didn't. Things had changed. Maybe Silvers himself, who was an entertainer in WWII, was more comfortable in a military role. Maybe America had changed? But, perhaps a deeper clue lies in the personality of Silvers himself.

In the 1950s he was one of the highest paid entertainers in America; but he had a dark secret. Like his character, he was a compulsive gambler and would stay at the craps table until he had lost everything and more. On one occasion, Silvers spent the entire night playing until he lost all his money and went through $1,000 in credit. He told the taxi driver "Don't wait for any lights and don't wait for a tip, I left it all at the table." It was a line worthy of *The Phil Silvers Show*, if it were written as a tragi-comedy by Samuel Beckett.

Cathy McGowan

Ready, Steady, Go!

Hosted by Cathy McGowan and Keith Fordyce
Ran from 9th August 1963 to 23rd December 1966

As Cathy MacGowan would say: "The weekend starts here." Introduced as the ultimate 60s pop show, presented by Keith Fordyce and Cathy MacGowan, *Ready, Steady, Go!* was a staple part of TV in the early part of the 1960s. It had a simple formula to showcase artists (usually miming) from both the UK and US in front of an audience who danced or stood around during the performances. MacGowan was a mini-skirted sixties icon, while Fordyce would have looked more at home as an assistant in a furniture shop. Still, it was a start and it pre-dated *Top of the Pops* (1964). Big names who appeared on *Ready, Steady, Go!*, included Dusty Springfield, The Animals, The Rolling Stones, The Beatles and Dave Berry. The theme tune was provided by Manfred Mann, namely the catchy *54321*.

Perhaps it was not the most inventive of music shows and suffered from the miming aspect which made most artists look ridiculous as they lip synced to a track which resounded around the huge space miles away from where they were standing. It was hardly definitive but was the first attempt on British TV (after *6-5 Special*) to provide a weekly showcase for the movers and shakers of popular music. The last show was broadcast on 23rd December 1966 and was called *Ready, Steady, Goes!* For all its failings, it was a landmark music programme which furthered the careers of many great British acts.

Overview of Radio Broadcasting

The biggest event in British radio in the early 1960s was one that could not be heard by the public, but would eventually change the way we listened to radio forever. In June 1962, the Pilkington Committee on Broadcasting published a report that would devolve BBC radio to the regions. Fearful of the impending creation of local commercial radio, the nation's broadcaster hoped to get a head start. Test closed-circuit broadcasts ran through to 1967 when BBC Radio Leicester launched. In the meantime the British public had to make do with three services, little changed since around the time of the Second World War. The Home Service, which evolved from the pre-war National Programme, featured news, entertainment and magazine programmes such as *Woman's Hour*. This was to become Radio 4. The Light Programme, launched in 1945, featured jazz and easy listening music as well as sport and light entertainment.

Broadcasting House in London

This was to become Radio 2. The Third Programme was the most highbrow of the three, playing classical music, this eventually became Radio 3. There was much to inform and entertain the listener and many have endured to this day. *Farming Today*, *The Archers*, *Any Questions?* and *In Touch* can still be heard. Other programmes seemed tired and staid and were soon to run their course. *Music While you Work*, *Housewife's Choice* and *The Dales* spoke more to an older generation than the baby boomers of the day. The last named programme, *The Dales*, had changed its name from *Mrs Dale's Diary* in 1962 and the linking narratives by Mrs Dale were dropped. This was in no small part due to the erratic behaviour of the star Ellis Powell, who struggled with alcohol addiction. On 19th February 1963, she was sacked and three months later died aged 57. The *Killing of Sister George*, a 1968 film starring Beryl Reid, is loosely based on her life. For pre-school children there was always *Listen With Mother*. Sport also featured prominently with *Test Match Special* bringing painterly descriptions of England cricket matches from around the globe. Silky voiced poet and cricket-lover John Arlott was the greatest of the commentators. The BBC was also keen on

Letter from America with Alistair Cooke

real life outside broadcasts; *Down Your Way*, a programme that toured the towns and villages of the UK, was hugely popular. What was sorely lacking in the Corporation's output was programming aimed at the youth market. There were two shows, *Pick of the Pops* and *Easy Beat*, which catered for the young, but very little else. In America, newscaster Don Gardiner interrupted the Doris Day song *Hooray for Hollywood* to announce that shots had been fired at the motorcade of President JFK. This was the first national broadcast bulletin of the news of the shooting. One programme which bridged the Atlantic and became compulsory listening for many was Alistair Cooke's *Letter from America*. In a world far less interconnected than today's, Cooke would broadcast weekly from his adopted New York. His broadcasts ranged from idle conversations with his local barkeeper to momentous events of the day.

Louie Louie

Performed by **The Kingsmen**

Written by **Richard Berry**

Originally released in 1957. The Kingsmen's version released in 1963

The Kingsmen

Possibly the most famous banned track in American history, *Louie Louie* was originally a 1957 song by Richard Berry. However, in 1963, The Kingsmen remade the song with some obscure and seemingly incomprehensible lyrics that *Ultimate Classic Rock* (a US rock radio show) deemed explicit. According to some, the lyrics alluded to casual sex; others heard at least one expletive. This led to a ban by many stations. When an individual complained to the acting Attorney General, Robert F. Kennedy, an FBI investigation was launched to figure out what exactly the song lyrics said. The FBI determined that "it was not possible to determine whether this recording is obscene." Like most songs that were banned throughout the history of music, the public rushed to buy the single and it reached No:1 in the Cashbox charts in America.

Be My Baby

Performed by **The Ronettes**

Recorded 29th July 1963

The Ronettes

The song was one of the defining rock'n roll songs of the 1960s advancing a new sound that changed popular music forever. It was sung by three young girls from New York's Spanish Harlem who came to be known as the Ronettes. They were sisters Estelle and Ronnie Bennett and their cousin, Nedra Talle. It is also part of the American soundtrack that marked a time when the nation was both optimistic and a bit more innocent prior to the shocking murder of a young and promising president, John F. Kennedy. But *Be My Baby* is also a story about the people who made the music; a story about the lives and careers of those involved with the Ronettes during the 1963-66 period and beyond. A few intense and difficult relationships followed, along with the demise of the Ronettes' group; ill health for one member and a prominent divorce for another. A protracted legal battle over royalties and licensing rights ensued.

Surfin' USA

Performed by **The Beach Boys**

Written by **Chuck Berry and Brian Wilson**

Released: 4th March 1963

The Beach Boys

In the early 1960s the Beach Boys became one of America's hottest and most successful groups, credited with inventing "California rock" and "sunshine pop." Along with the Beatles, they also pushed the boundaries of contemporary music on a new and imaginative front of songwriting and pop composition. Their music was happy, fun-loving and filled with beautiful harmonies. *Surfin' USA* was a reworking of Chuck Berry's *Sweet Sixteen* and is a catalogue of California surfing spots. Its lyrics "If everybody had an ocean, across the U.S.A, then everybody'd be surfin' Like Californ-I-A" were aspirational especially to those who lived miles from the warm seas off the West Coast. The song reached Number 2 in the US charts, but only number 34 in the UK. I guess the cold waters of Skegness were less appealing than the golden beaches of Californ-I-A.

Gerry And The Pacemakers

You'll Never Walk Alone

Performed by Gerry And The Pacemakers

Written by Richard Rodgers and Oscar Hammerstein II

The song began life on Broadway as part of the Rodgers and Hammerstein 1945 show, *Carousel*. It was an instant hit, probably because the song's message of triumph in times of adversity spoke to the wartime crowds of April 1945. It remained popular throughout the '50s, with artists including Frank Sinatra and Elvis Presley releasing covers. Then in 1963, a recording by Merseybeat band, Gerry And The Pacemakers, brought the song to the doorstep of Liverpool FC. At that time, Liverpool's Anfield Stadium was one of the few football grounds to have a PA system. The Top Ten in the charts would be played before each match. *You'll Never Walk Alone* stayed at No. 1 in the charts for about four weeks in 1963, by which time it had become Liverpool FC's signature tune. Its status as Liverpool's anthem was cemented when manager Bill Shankley chose it as one of his records on *Desert Island Discs*.

The Dave Clark Five

Glad All Over

Performed by The Dave Clark Five

Written by Dave Clark and Mike Smith

Released: 15th November 1963

Billboard said of the song that "here's a rocking, romping group vocal effort much akin to the Liverpool sound and the Beatles' school," stating that the song has a "solid beat and echo quality." It was a slow burner of a song and was only the 58th best selling single of 1963. By the end of the following year it had sold over 1 million copies in the UK alone, ending up as the second best selling single behind the Beatles' *I Want to Hold Your Hand*. South London football club Crystal Palace adopted the song as their anthem. It is played at the start of all home games, and after full-time (when Palace win). The chorus is played after home goals, after the goal scorer's name is read out. It is also sung by fans as a chant. On Saturday 10th February 1968, The Dave Clark Five played *Glad All Over* live at Crystal Palace's home, Selhurst Park.

The Beatles

She Loves You

Written and Performed by The Beatles

Released: 23rd August 1963

From the opening drum roll, *She Loves You* takes no prisoners, charging into its indelible "yeah, yeah, yeah" hook; it was George Martin's successful brainstorm to move the chorus to the very beginning of the song. Although lyrically it was, like most of Lennon-McCartney's early compositions, an elementary boy-girl situation heavy on the pronouns, there was a twist in that it was related in the third person. Instead of telling a girl how much they were in love, they were scolding a friend for throwing away the love of a lifetime. What won over listeners' hearts, though, were the use of block harmonies. Lennon and McCartney were also proud of ending the choruses on a sixth chord, which they initially believed had never been done before. It fell to producer George Martin to inform them that others had used it, such as Glenn Miller, but that didn't take away from its freshness in a rock context.

Cliff Richards and The Shadows

Summary Holiday
Summer Holiday
By Cliff Richards and The Shadows
Released: 8th February 1963

In 1961 Cliff Richard starred in his first major film, *The Young Ones*. The soundtrack, co-written by members of Cliff's backing group, The Shadows, spawned several hits including the title track. The Shadows rhythm guitarist Bruce Welch and drummer Brian Bennett wrote this sing-along for Richard's next movie, *Summer Holiday*. Welch recalled "We were in pantomime in Stockton-on-Tees when we got a synopsis for the next movie. It said "four or five guys hire a London bus and drive through Europe". That was it. Our drummer Brian Bennett was in the orchestra pit. I sang we're all going on a summer holiday" Brian wrote "We're going where the sun shines brightly. We're going where the sea is blue." It took us about half an hour to write." He then went on to claim that the song changed society, which was a bit OTT, but it was a nice fresh ditty that was full of youthful exuberance.

The Crystals

Da Doo Ron Ron
Performed by The Crystals
Written by Jeff Barry, Ellie Greenwich and Phil Spector

Phil Spector produced this song, marking his first real "Wall of Sound" production. It provided the template for his unique studio sound that he would replicate on other classic songs. He recorded it at Gold Star Studios in Los Angeles, packing all the musicians into a tiny room. Spector was meticulous about microphone placement. He recorded the song in mono, which meant that every instrument was coming out of both speakers at full force. Spector wasn't big on editing or post-production, so he spent a lot of his studio time having the musicians run through the track before he would roll tape. Typically, he would have the guitarists play for a while as he worked out the song, then bring in pianos, bass and drums. Vocals were recorded in an echo chamber located behind the control room at Gold Star. Among the backing singers was one of Spector's favourites, namely Cher.

The Beatles

I Want To Hold Your Hand
By The Beatles
Released: 29th November 1963

With advance orders exceeding one million copies in the United Kingdom, it would ordinarily have gone straight to the top of the British record charts on its day of release had it not been blocked by the group's first million seller *She Loves You*, the Beatles' previous UK single, which was having a resurgent spell in the top position following intense media coverage of the group. Taking two weeks to dislodge its predecessor, *I Want To Hold Your Hand* stayed at number one for five weeks and remained in the UK top fifty for twenty-one weeks in total. It was also the group's first American number one, entering the Billboard Hot 100 chart on 18th January 1964 at number forty-five and starting the British invasion of the American music industry. By 1st February it had held the number one spot for seven weeks, before being replaced by *She Loves You*, a reverse scenario of what had occurred in Britain.

Top of the Pops in 1963

There were 18 number one records in 1963 in the UK single charts published by the NME. The best selling single of the year was *She Loves You* by The Beatles.

	Weeks at number one
Return to Sender / Elvis Presley From 27th December 1962 for 1 week	I
The Next Time/Bachelor Boy / Cliff Richard and The Shadows From 3rd January 1963 for 3 weeks	III
Dance On / The Shadows From 24th January 1963 for 1 week	I
Diamonds / Jet Harris and Tony Meehan From 31st January 1963 for 3 weeks	III
The Wayward Wind / Frank Ifield From 21st February 1963 for 3 weeks	III
Summer Holiday / Cliff Richard and The Shadows From 14th March 1963 for 2 weeks then 4th April for 1 week	III
Foot Tapper / The Shadows From 28th March 1963 for 1 week	I
How Do You Do It? / Gerry and the Pacemakers From 11th April 1963 for 3 weeks	III
From Me To You / The Beatles From 2nd May 1963 for 7 weeks	IIIIIII
I Like It / Gerry and the Pacemakers From 20th June 1963 for 4 weeks	IIII
Confessin' / Frank Ifield From 18th July 1963 for 2 weeks	II
(You're the) Devil in Disguise / Elvis Presley From 1st August 1963 for 1 week	I
Sweets For My Sweet / The Searchers From 8th August 1963 for 2 weeks	II
Bad To Me / Billy J. Kramer and the Dakotas From 22nd August 1963 for 3 weeks	III
She Loves You / The Beatles From 12th September 1963 for 4 weeks then 28th November for 2 weeks	IIIIII
Do You Love Me / Brian Poole and the Tremeloes From 10th October 1963 for 3 weeks	III
You'll Never Walk Alone / Gerry and the Pacemakers From 31st October 1963 for 4 weeks	IIII
I Want To Hold Your Hand / The Beatles From 12th December 1963 for 3 weeks	III

Bob Dylan Live

Bob Dylan

CBS Records recorded Bob Dylan's 26th October 1963 performance at New York City's venerable Carnegie Hall for a proposed live LP provisionally titled *In Concert*, pressing acetates and even printing cardboard sleeves before abruptly scuttling the project for good. The assassination of John F. Kennedy altered most people's plans, of course and legend also has it that execs were flummoxed by a six-minute spoken monologue entitled *Last Thoughts on Woody Guthrie*, one of several cuts added to the album from an April 12th gig at New York's Town Hall. Bootleg versions circulated for years, and in 1991 Columbia officially issued two cuts - the ripped-from-the-headlines *Who Killed Davey Moore?* and the satirical *Talkin' John Birch Society Blues* as part of the box set *The Bootleg Series 1-3*. Finally, in conjunction with the 2005 release of Martin Scorsese's documentary portrait *No Direction Home*, the label released a beautifully packaged six-song promotional disc in the vein of the original *In Concert* cover but still frustratingly incomplete. What's left is an extraordinary record of the young Dylan at the pinnacle of his craft, in transition from the protest anthems on which his early fame rested towards the deeply personal and hauntingly poetic songs that remain his greatest legacy. From a fiery rendition of *The Times They Are a-Changin'* to a jaw-droppingly beautiful *Boots of Spanish Leather*, this is music that transcends space and time. When Dylan withdrew from public life after a motorcycle accident in 1966, other singers started recording his songs. This led to an increase in demand for the original work and more bootleg albums were released.

The Inaugural Leeds International Pianoforte Competition

The competition in Leeds Town Hall

On the 23rd September 1963, delight was exceeded only by surprise in Leeds at the victory in the International Piano Competition of a local boy, Michael Roll. At the age of 17, he was the youngest of the 94 qualifiers. Until this victory at Leeds, he was not yet committed to a career as a pianist, but was intending to follow in his father's footsteps as a doctor. Out of the 10 concertos which were the test-pieces for the third and final stage of the competition on Saturday night, he chose Schumann's. Roll certainly made it the most rewarding musical experience of the evening even though it had already been played by one of the other three finalists. It was a robust and animated performance, well shaped, with a splendid rhythmic impetus in all three movements. This was not at all easy to sustain in this piece, as had conspicuously been demonstrated to the audience earlier by Armenta Adams, a contestant from New York. She had taken the first two movements too slowly and was in continual trouble with her scheme of tempi. Adams was more successful in the last movement, livelier and more stable and was unlucky to lose her way. John Pritchard, conducting the Royal Liverpool Philharmonic Orchestra, quickly got her restarted and she finished well. However, she placed fourth of the four finalists. Michael Roll went on to have a long and distinguished career, playing with the London Philharmonic, London Symphony and the Boston Symphony Orchestras.

The Eurovision Scandal

On the 23rd March 1963 at The BBC Television Centre, White City, London

The Eurovision Song Contest's foundation stemmed from a desire to promote cooperation between European countries in the years following the Second World War through cross-border television broadcasts, leading to the founding of the European Broadcasting Union (EBU) in 1950. The word "Eurovision" was coined by British journalist George Campey in the London Evening Standard in 1951. The honour of hosting the 1963 song contest was handed over by the French, who had won it in 1960 and 1962, to the United Kingdom. The main reason for this was that France did not want to host the song contest so soon after holding it twice in Cannes in 1959 and 1961. Big international stars took part in the year's competition, like Esther Ofarim (who was Israeli) for Switzerland, Nana Mouskouri (who hailed from Greece) for Luxembourg and Francoise Hardy (who was born in Paris) for Monaco. Host Broadcaster, the BBC, tried a novel approach for the presentation of the contest. All songs were performed in one studio, but the audience was located in another. Each song had its own unique staging and the changes of set were done very swiftly. As a result of this, rumours began to circulate that the performances were pre-recorded which turned out to be totally untrue. The Norwegian head of jury was still busy adding up the individual votes of the 20 jury members when called in by the presenter Katie Boyle. Struck by panic he delivered their results in the wrong format. In accordance with the rules, Mrs. Boyle told the TV audience that she would come back to the Norwegian jury after all the other countries had voted. When the final results came in from the Norwegian jury, they were noticeably different from the earlier ones and gave the victory to Norway's Nordic neighbour, Denmark (represented by husband and wife team Grethe and Jørgen Ingmann) denying the victory to Switzerland. This subsequently led to accusations that the Norway jury had deliberately altered their votes. The British entry was Northern Ireland's Ronnie Carroll's rendition of *Say Wonderful Things*. It finished fourth. Finland, Sweden, The Netherlands and Norway received "nul points." Following the contest, Grethe and Jørgen Ingmann recorded and released the winning song *Dansevise* in English with the title *I Loved You*. It was not a hit in the UK, but reached number seven in the Norwegian charts. Of all the artists who performed at the contest Nana Mouskouri went on to be the most successful. She is one of the best-selling artists of all time, largely due to the fact that she sang in a wide range of languages. She also had a distinctive style, often introducing her songs, painting a picture for the audience.

UK entrant Norman Carroll

Winners Jørgen and Grethe Ingmann

Luxembourg entrant Nana Mouskouri

1963 was a significant year in literature, with many notable works published across different genres. One of the most influential works of the year was Sylvia Plath's posthumously published collection of poems, *Ariel*. Plath's hauntingly beautiful and confessional poetry has since become a staple of contemporary poetry and a seminal examination of the complexities of mental illness and personal struggles. Another notable work from 1963 was the science fiction novel *Cat's Cradle* by Kurt Vonnegut. He explores themes of science, religion and human nature in a satirical and thought-provoking way, solidifying Vonnegut's place as one of the most important literary voices of the 20th century. 1963 also saw the publication of Sylvia Plath's semi-autobiographical novel *The Bell Jar*, which is now considered a classic of feminist literature. It tells the story of a young woman's struggle with mental illness and societal expectations in the 1950s. Other notable works of fiction from 1963 include *A Moveable Feast* by Ernest

Author Kurt Vonnegut

Pop artist Roy Lichtenstein

Hemingway, *The Sailor Who Fell from Grace with the Sea* by Yukio Mishima and *The Group* by Mary McCarthy. The year also saw the deaths of two great British writer and thinkers - Aldous Huxley and C.S. Lewis. Pop Art continued to gain momentum in 1963, with key figures such as Andy Warhol, Roy Lichtenstein and Claes Oldenburg producing some of their most iconic works. Warhol's *Campbell's Soup Cans* and Lichtenstein's *Whaam!* are prime examples of the movement's focus on popular culture and commercial imagery. The term "minimalism" was first used in 1963 to describe a group of artists including Donald Judd, Dan Flavin and Carl Andre, who emphasised simple forms and utilised industrial materials. The movement was a reaction against Abstract Expressionism and sought to create a more objective and rational art. The term minimalism is also used to describe a trend in design and architecture, wherein the subject is reduced to its necessary elements. Minimalist architectural designers focused on the connection between two perfect planes, elegant lighting and the void spaces left by the removal of three-dimensional shapes. Though conceived in the early 1960s it did not become popular until the 1980s, most notably in London and New York. Fluxus was a loose collective of artists and musicians who sought to break down the boundaries between art and life. In 1963, they organised a series of events in Wiesbaden, Germany, known as the Fluxus Festival. These events included performances, happenings, and installations that often involved audience participation. Performance art emerged as a distinct genre in the early 1960s, with key figures such as Yoko Ono, Allan Kaprow and Carolee Schneemann pushing the boundaries of what was considered art. In 1963, Kaprow organised an event called *18 Happenings in 6 Parts*, which took place at the Reuben Gallery in New York City.

American painter Allan Kaprow

The Spy Who Came In From The Cold

Author: John le Carré   Published: September 1963

The story follows Alec Leamas, a British spy who is sent to East Germany to work as a double agent. Leamas is tasked with convincing the East Germans that he has become disillusioned with the British intelligence service and is willing to betray his country. However, as the plot unfolds, it becomes clear that nothing is as it seems. Leamas is manipulated by his superiors and forced to make difficult choices in order to achieve his objectives. Along the way, he develops a relationship with a woman named Liz, who works for the East Germans.

The novel is notable for its gritty, realistic portrayal of the world of espionage. It is a stark departure from the glamorous image of spies often portrayed in popular culture. It was a critical and commercial success upon its release, and is considered a classic of the spy genre. In 1965, it was made into a film starring Richard Burton and Claire Bloom.

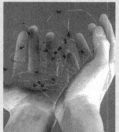

Cat's Cradle

Author: Kurt Vonnegut   First published in 1963

The story is narrated by a writer who sets out to research the life of Felix Hoenikker, a scientist who played a key role in the development of the atomic bomb. However, as the narrator delves deeper into Hoenikker's life, he discovers a substance called Ice-9 that could destroy all life on Earth. The novel is a commentary on the Cold War and the fear of nuclear annihilation that permeated American society in the 1960s. Vonnegut uses dark humour and satire to critique the arms race and the idea that technology will solve all of humanity's problems. The characters in the novel are flawed and often absurd, highlighting the insanity of the world they inhabit. Through the use of science fiction elements, Vonnegut explores the dangers of human ambition and the unintended consequences of scientific advances. The novel also touches on themes of religion, power and the human condition.

The Collector

Author: John Fowles   Published: May 1963

The novel follows the story of Frederick Clegg, a socially awkward man who becomes obsessed with Miranda Grey, a young art student he admires from afar. After winning a large sum of money, Clegg decides to kidnap Miranda and keep her in his basement, hoping that she will eventually fall in love with him. The novel is told from the alternating perspectives of both characters, as Miranda tries to escape while Clegg struggles with his own feelings of inadequacy and social isolation. The novel explores themes of obsession, power and control, as well as the complex relationship between captor and captive. Fowles uses the narrative structure to create tension and suspense, as readers are unsure of the outcome for Miranda and Clegg. The book and the film adaptation gained notoriety when several serial killers claimed that the book provided their inspiration. In 1984, multiple killer Christopher Wilder had *The Collector* in his possession when he was gunned down by police in New Hampshire.

Planet of the Apes (in French: La Planète des Singes)
Author: Pierre Boulle   First published in 1963

Planet of the Apes is a science fiction novel where, on another planet, great apes are the dominant and civilised species. The novel begins with Jinn and Phyllis sailing through space when they discover a manuscript in a bottle. The manuscript is the testament of Ulysse Merou, part of a French space expedition launched to find life on other planets. The expedition consists of Professor Antelle, a physician named Arhur Levain and Ulysse himself, an aspiring journalist. They arrive on an Earth-like planet in the Betelgeuse system, after a voyage of two years. They name the planet "Soror". There, they are stunned to discover human beings living totally naked like animals in the forest. These humans cannot speak and do not have any recognisable human customs apart from sexual activity.   Ulysse and his comrades are captured and taken to a lab to be tested, studied and experimented on by the apes. The book was made into a film in 1968 starring Charlton Heston becoming a global media franchise including books, TV series and comics.

The Bell Jar
Author: Sylvia Plath   Published: January 1963

This semi-autobiographical novel, set in the 1950s, tells the story of Esther Greenwood, a young woman who is struggling with mental illness. She is a bright, ambitious college student who has won a prestigious internship at a fashion magazine in New York City. However, as she struggles to fit in with this superficial world, Esther begins to experience a deep sense of isolation and despair. Throughout the book, Esther's mental health deteriorates further as she becomes increasingly suicidal. Eventually, she is admitted to a mental hospital, where she undergoes electroconvulsive therapy. *The Bell Jar* is a powerful and deeply moving exploration of the experience of mental illness, as well as a commentary on the oppressive social expectations that women faced in the mid-twentieth century. Despite its dark subject matter, it is a compelling and ultimately hopeful book, offering a message of resilience and survival in the face of adversity.

On Her Majesty's Secret Service
Author: Ian Fleming   Published: 1st April 1963

The book, the eleventh in the James Bond series, follows 007 as he investigates the mysterious activities of a criminal organisation called SPECTRE, which is led by the enigmatic Ernst Stavro Blofeld. Bond's investigation leads him to Switzerland, where he meets Tracy, a beautiful and troubled young woman, who becomes his ally and eventually his love interest. As he delves deeper into SPECTRE's activities, he uncovers a plot to unleash a deadly virus that could wipe out humanity. Bond must race against time to foil SPECTRE's plans, all the while dodging their deadly agents and grappling with his own personal demons. *On Her Majesty's Secret Service* is widely regarded as one of Fleming's finest Bond novels, featuring a gripping plot, intense action sequences and a complex and nuanced portrayal of Bond himself. The novel also marked a significant departure from the formulaic nature of earlier Bond books, incorporating more character development and emotional depth.

Where The Wild Things Are

Written and illustrated by Maurice Sendak   Published: 13th November 1963

The story follows a young boy named Max who, after being sent to his room without supper, imagines a wild jungle inhabited by fantastical creatures known as "Wild Things". Max becomes their king and leads them in a wild rumpus, but eventually decides to return home. The book has been beloved by generations of readers for its vivid illustrations and imaginative storytelling. It has won numerous awards, including the Caldecott Medal for "the most distinguished American picture book for children" in 1964. At its heart, it is a story about the power of imagination and the importance of self-expression. It encourages children to embrace their wild side, to let their imaginations run free and not be afraid of their emotions. This timeless classic has spawned many animated films. It was also parodied in a 2005 episode of the Simpsons, *The Girl Who Slept Too Little* in which *Where The Wild Things Are* was replaced by *The Land Of The Beasts*.

Hop on Pop

Written and illustrated by Theodor Seuss Geisel (aka Dr. Seuss)

First published on the 13th November 1963, the book is a simple and fun read, designed to help children learn basic reading skills through rhyming and repetition. It consists of short, simple sentences and rhyming words, which make it easy for young readers to follow along. The illustrations are also colourful and playful, adding to the overall charm of the book. The book's main focus is on word families, where each page features a different set of words that all rhyme with each other. For example, "UP PUP Pup is up. CUP PUP Pup in cup" and "HOP POP We like to hop. We like to hop on top of Pop."

Hop on Pop is a great book for young children who are just starting to learn how to read. It is easy to follow, fun to read and provides a great foundation for building reading skills. Dr. Seuss's unique writing style and creative illustrations have made this book a timeless classic that continues to be read by parents to young children and by the youngsters themselves.

The Gashlycrumb Tinies

Written and illustrated by Edward Gory   First published in 1963

The book is an abecedarium, one that utilises each letter of the alphabet for its segments usually written in alphabetical order. Although the style of writing is mainly reserved for religious texts, Gory uses it in this darkly humorous work. The book features twenty-six children, each representing a letter of the alphabet, who meet their untimely demise in various macabre and absurd ways. The book's illustrations are black and white, and the text is written in rhyming couplets. Each page features a child and a short verse describing their fate, such as "A is for Amy who fell down the stairs" or "Y is for Yorick whose head was knocked in." Despite its macabre subject matter, *The Gashlycrumb Tinies* is beloved by many for its dark humour and Gorey's distinctive drawing style. The book has been referenced in popular culture, including in Tim Burton's film *The Melancholy Death of Oyster Boy & Other Stories*.

Barefoot in the Park

Written by Neil Simon
Starring Robert Redford and Elizabeth Astley
Premiered on 23rd October 1963 at The Biltmore Theatre on Broadway

Playwright Neil Simon

Corie (Astley) and Paul Bratter (Redford) are a newly-wed couple. For their first home, they live in an apartment on the top floor of a brownstone building in New York City. Corie is optimistic about their future together. Paul, the more anxious and grounded half of the couple, worries about the various flaws in the apartment such as a hole in the skylight, their leaky closet and the lack of a bathtub. Shortly after moving in, Corie attempts to set her mother up with their eccentric neighbour Mr. Velasco. During the course of four days, the couple learn to live together while facing the usual daily ups-and-downs. Corie wants Paul to become more easy-going: for example, to run "barefoot in the park". The New York Times called it 'one of the funniest comedies ever.' On the basis of this and other strong reviews and even stronger word of mouth, the Broadway production became a sold-out hit, causing the Biltmore Theatre to double the number of staff in its box-office to deal with the demand for tickets. Redford, best known as a movie actor, starred in a film version of the play in 1967 alongside Jane Fonda. Redford and Fonda would appear in front of the camera again some fifty years later in the critically acclaimed *Our Souls at Night* (2017).

War Requiem

Composed by Benjamin Britten
German debut: 6th June 1963 in Munich

Benjamin Britten

Benjamin Britten's *War Requiem* is a mass commemorating those who died during two world wars, but the work also serves as a call for peace. It is considered to be one of the most important choral works to address the wars of the 20th century. The passionate pacifist composed the piece as a commission to mark the consecration of England's new Coventry Cathedral, also known as St. Michael's. It premiered there on 30th May 1962. "My subject is War, and the pity of War / ... All a poet can do today is warn." Benjamin Britten placed these words by British poet Wilfred Owen at the beginning of his requiem, and interspersed his Latin Mass for the Dead with lines from nine poems about war by Owen. For Britten, Owen's poems were about the rejection of destructive forces in the world. The composer viewed them as a kind of commentary on the text of the Mass for the Dead. While *War Requiem* mourns the countless deaths during the war, its purpose was also to be a sign of reconciliation between Great Britain and Germany. Britten was convinced that rapprochement was possible only when the nations maintained a dialogue. Those convictions were reflected at the premiere of the work, where German baritone Dietrich Fischer-Dieskau sang in Coventry at Britten's request. He reprised his performance for the German premiere in Munich in 1963. The opera was made into a film in 1989 by Derek Jarman. It continues to be performed to this day at venues such as St. Paul's Cathedral.

John Masefield, Poet Laureate (served 1930-1967)

John Masefield

Masefield was the longest serving Poet Laureate to serve entirely within the 20th century. His 37 years of service was only beaten by Alfred, Lord Tennyson who held the post between 1850-1892. By the 1950s Masefield seemed from a bygone era as traditional poetry had fallen out of public favour, whilst more modernist poets such as Sylvia Plath and Stevie Smith were gaining more traction. The emerging Beat Generation of poets such as Ginsburg, Carr and Huncke seemed to speak more to the youth of the day than did the rather staid Masefield. Still, he took his job seriously and acted as all good Poets Laureate do and wrote poems for the court, in his case the House of Windsor. Rather quaintly, Masefield would send his poems to the Times of London for their approval with a stamped addressed envelope for their response. Even though he seemed more like a 19th century poet than most of his contemporaries, many of his poems still stand the test of time. His *Sonnets and Poems* written in the midst of World War I and *A Generation Risen* written during World War II defined him as a chronicler of British 20th century history. He is one of the few poets to have written during both wars. On 25th November 1963, John Masefield's memorial poem to John F. Kennedy was published in the London Times.

The Role of Poet Laureate Through The Ages

The monarch of the day bestows the honorary position of Poet Laureate, currently on the advice of the prime minister. There are no specific duties to the role, although it is expected that the holder produces original verse to commemorate significant national occasions. The first official Poet Laureate was John Dryden who was appointed by Charles II in 1668. Until Andrew Motion was appointed in 1999 the laureateship was held for life; subsequently the position has been offered for a fixed term of 10 years. Other notable Poets Laureate included William Wordsworth (1843-1850), Sir John Betjeman (1972-1984) and Ted Hughes (1984-1998). The actor Daniel Day-Lewis's father, Cecil, was also Poet Laureate from 1968 to 1972. It was only in 2009 that the first woman, Carol Ann Duffy, was offered the role. She was also the first Scot.

Sir John Betjeman

The role of Poet Laureate is not a money spinner; Andrew Motion and Carol Ann Duffy were offered annual salaries of £5,750 per year. However, in a quirky tradition dating back to Charles I, the holder also receives a barrel of sherry.

Carol Ann Duffy

The Mercury-Atlas 9 Solo Orbital Mission

Astronaut Leroy Gordon Cooper Jr.

On May 15th 1963, astronaut Leroy Gordon "Gordo" Cooper Jr. became the first American to spend over 24 hours in space during the Mercury-Atlas 9 mission. This groundbreaking mission was a major achievement for the US space program, and helped pave the way for future manned spaceflight missions. During the Mercury-Atlas 9 mission, Cooper orbited the Earth 22 times over the course of 34 hours, travelling a distance of over 470,000 nautical miles. He conducted a series of scientific experiments, including measuring the effects of prolonged spaceflight on the human body and testing new communication systems. However, the mission wasn't without its challenges. Just a few hours into the flight, Cooper's automatic stabilisation system failed, leaving him to manually control the spacecraft's orientation for the remainder of the mission. And during re-entry, a malfunction caused the heat shield to loosen, putting Cooper's life in danger. Despite these obstacles, Cooper successfully landed in the Pacific Ocean, where he was picked up by a US Navy helicopter. His successful mission marked a major milestone in the space race between the US and Soviet Union, and cemented his place in history as one of America's greatest astronauts.

Valentina Tereshkova | The First Woman In Space

Cosmonaut Valentina Tereshkova

In 1963, the world was captivated by two historic space missions. Gordon Cooper's Atlas 9 mission was a remarkable achievement for NASA, marking the final orbital mission of the Mercury program. But what many people don't realise is that just a few days later, the Soviet Union launched Vostok 6 sending the first woman, Valentina Tereshkova, into space. The Vostok 6 mission was a groundbreaking moment in space exploration, and yet it is often overlooked in history books. Tereshkova's mission was a triumph for the Soviet Union, and was a critical moment in the Cold War space race. But more than that, it was an inspiration to women around the world who saw in Tereshkova a symbol of what was possible. Despite facing numerous challenges and potential dangers, Tereshkova completed her mission successfully. She spent almost three days in space, orbiting the Earth 48 times. Her journey paved the way for future generations of female astronauts. The Vostok 6 mission was a pivotal moment in the history of space exploration, and it deserves to be celebrated alongside other great achievements in human spaceflight.

Félicette | The First And Only Cat In Space

This mission into space did not garner the media interest generated by the two on the opposite page, nonetheless it was an important milestone for France and its newly established civilian space agency CERMA (third in the world after the Soviet Union and the US). Six years earlier, the Soviet Union had sent Laika, a stray dog found on the streets of Moscow, into space. The French decided to send a cat. Félicitte was one of 14 stray cats found in Paris used in the programme. On 18th October 1963 she became the first and only feline to ever visit space. She was propelled by a Véronique AG1 rocket to a height of 157 kilometres (almost 100 miles). She was subjected to 9.5 g's of force as her rocket accelerated up to six times the speed of sound on a mission lasting only 15 minutes. The modern animal rights movement didn't start until the 1970s so the use of animals for this kind of scientific endeavour was more or less tolerated in the

Photo of Félicette with thank you note

1960s. Over and above the stresses of the journey, Félicitte had electrodes implanted into her skull so her neurological activity could be monitored during the mission. She survived the flight but was sadly euthanised 2 months later in order to examine her brain. Her contribution to space flight has only recently been recognised with a bronze statue of her likeness on display at the International Space University near Strasbourg in France.

The World's Largest Radio Telescope

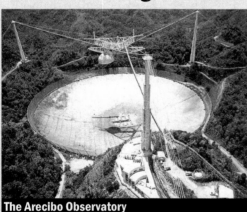

The Arecibo Observatory

One of the most famous scientific devices of the 20th century was the Arecibo Telescope, which was located in Puerto Rico. Completed in November 1963, it had a 1,000-foot-wide dish built into a natural sinkhole. For more than 50 years it was the biggest single-dish radio telescope in the world. The main use of the telescope was radio astronomy, which allowed scientists to examine radio waves generated by galaxies, stars, and other celestial objects. It was also used in the SETI programme, the search for extraterrestrial intelligence. The Arecibo Telescope made a number of ground-breaking discoveries during the course of its lifetime, including the identification of the first binary pulsar providing compelling proof for the existence of gravitational waves. Sadly the telescope's support cables sustained irreversible damage in 2020 causing the central receiver structure to collapse into the dish. The site was decommissioned the following year. The deactivation of the telescope signalled the end of an era in astronomy and the loss of a cherished scientific monument. It was announced to much regret and dismay. The dish was also immortalised in the climax of the 1995 James Bond movie *Goldeneye* (starring Pierce Brosnan), when Bond and villain Alec Trevelyan battled to the death.

A Year of Firsts for Organ Transplantation

The year 1963 was a watershed point in medical history for organ transplantation. Physicians successfully transplanted a human liver and a human lung for the first time, extending the possibility for life-saving treatments. These accomplishments heralded a new age of medical innovation in which the boundaries of what might be accomplished through surgery were fast being stretched. The accomplishments of 1963, however, were not without controversy. They raised challenging ethical considerations concerning the use of human organs and the boundaries of medical research.

The World's First Liver Transplant | 1st March 1963

Dr. Thomas Starzl, a pioneering transplant surgeon, performed the first successful liver transplant on 1st March 1963, at the University of Colorado School of Medicine. Bennie Solis, a three-year-old boy, was the patient. He had biliary atresia, a disorder that results in clogged bile ducts which damages the liver and finally leads it to fail. The donor liver was taken from a youngster who had died from a brain injury, and the operation was carried out by a team of surgeons. Despite initial success, Solis experienced a number of side effects, such as pneumonia and sepsis, which ultimately caused his death little over a year later. Yet, the procedure was an important turning point in medical history since it proved that it was possible to transplant a crucial organ and opened the door for later developments in liver transplantation. Dr. Starzl continued to perfect his procedures and improve outcomes for liver transplant

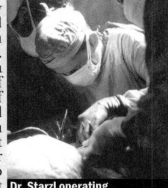
Dr. Starzl operating

patients after the successful transplant. He went on to execute countless additional transplants, establishing himself as a pioneer in the field of this type of surgery. Due to the pioneering work of Dr. Starzl and other medical pioneers, liver transplantation is now a reasonably frequent treatment, with thousands of successful transplants performed worldwide each year.

The World's First Lung Transplant | 11th June 1963

The date was the 11th June 1963, and the University of Mississippi Medical Center was gearing up for a revolutionary operation that would test the boundaries of contemporary medicine. John Russell, a life-sentenced murderer, was taken to the hospital with a long list of diseases that had him gasping for air and terrified for his life. Despite his condition, he accepted to be the world's first lung transplant recipient. The team, led by surgeon James Hardy, moved fast to get a healthy lung from a recently deceased heart attack patient. After the operation, however, they discovered that Russell's cancer had progressed beyond the lung meaning the transplant would not save his life but would instead improve his breathing. Russell had some respite after the operation before dying of renal failure 18 days later. The innovative procedure exposed medical technology's shortcomings at the time, such as inconsistent blood banking and minimal lab assistance. It did, however, lay the path for future advances in organ transplantation and motivated many participating in the procedure to become medical pioneers.

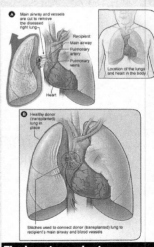
The lung transplant process

The World's First Computer Mouse

The British engineer Ralph Benjamin was the first to invent a pointing device for computers back in 1946 as part of a military project for a radar plotting system. This, however, was to become known as a trackball where the user controls the pointer by rotating a solid ball that is held in a captive socket. The invention of what we know today as the computer mouse is credited to the American engineer Douglas Engelbart. In 1963, he was leading the Augmentation Research Center at the Stanford

Douglas Engelbart's Mouse

Research Institute tasked with developing new tools and techniques to augment human intelligence. In November 1963, whilst attending a computer graphics conference in Reno, he jotted down ideas in his notebook for something called 'a bug'. It would be an object that has 2 wheels at right angles to each other and a 'drop point' (in essence a button). The object could be moved around a flat surface with its position being translated on to a screen. Unlike a stylus, if you let go, the object and pointer would stay where it is. In 1964, alongside engineer Bill English, Engelbart built the first prototype which they christened 'the mouse' due to the cord at the rear of the device resembling a tail. Engelbart would go on to publicly demonstrate the mouse in 1968 in what became known as 'The Mother of all Demos' which showcased many of the fundamental elements of modern personal computing that would later influence the design of the Apple Macintosh and Microsoft Windows.

Hypertext and The Origins of the Internet

The definition of hypertext is text that is presented on a computer screen or other electronic device with references (hyperlinks) to other content that the reader may view immediately. Hyperlinks connect hypertext documents and are often triggered by a mouse click, key press, or screen touch. The origins of hypertext can be traced back to a short story published in 1941 by Jorge Borges entitled *The Garden of Forking Paths*. In addition, an article in 1945 by the American engineer Vannevar Bush discussed the creation of a hypertext device called a Memex, but it was never built. It did, however, serve as

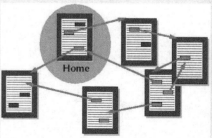
Documents connected by hyperlinks

the inspiration to Ted Nelson who is credited with coining the terms 'hypertext' and 'hypermedia' in 1963 as part of his 'Project Xanadu' which involved using linked content. The diagram shows how specific links embedded within the text of the document takes you to another document in a non-linear fashion. It was this hypertext functionality that Tim Berners-Lee would use as a significant component of his work in creating the World Wide Web in the late 1980s. It is also worth noting that Douglas Engelbart (see above) was separately working on a hypertext interface as part of his NLS (oN-Line System) at the same time as Ted Nelson. He demonstrated this to the public as part of his 1968 'Mother of all Demos'. Ted Nelson is also credited with creating the words *transclusion, virtuality* and *intertwingularity*; the latter meaning the complexity of interrelations in human knowledge.

The Mellotron

A Mellotron Mark VI

The Mellotron is an electro-mechanical musical instrument invented and manufactured from 1963 onward in Birmingham, England. It is effectively an early form of sampler. As opposed to a piano where a felt hammer strikes a string when you press a key, the Mellotron works by the key activating a mechanism where a length of magnetic tape pushes against a capstan, which drags it across a playback head. This plays the 'sample' sound recorded on to that portion of the tape. When the key is released, a spring retracts the tape to its original position. To hear different sounds, different parts of the tape are played. It was originally marketed for home use with celebrities including bandleader Eric Robinson, magician David Nixon and Princess Margaret listed among notable early customers. It wasn't until the mid sixties that musicians started to incorporate the Mellotron in their recordings. One of the most notable early uses of the instrument was in the intro to *Strawberry Fields Forever* by The Beatles, released in 1967. It gained further popularity in the 1970s as bands in the progressive rock movement such as Genesis and King Crimson incorporated the Mellotron. Its use eventually declined in the 1980's due to the introduction of more modern polyphonic synthesisers and samplers. However bands such as Oasis, who used the Mellotron for the cello sounds in their hit *Wonderwall*, and Radiohead, who used it in their album *OK Computer*, helped regain the instruments popularity. Production of the Mellotron, which had ceased in 1986, was resurrected in 2007.

The Moog Synthesiser

Bob Moog with some of his synthesisers

In 1963, Robert "Bob" Moog was working towards a PhD in engineering physics at Cornell University in the USA. He had also been designing and selling Theremins, an unusual musical instrument controlled by the musician moving their hands between two metal antennae to control the frequency and volume of the sound produced. Whilst at a music trade fair in New York he met the composer Herb Deutsch who had been making music using a theremin and tape recorder which involved time consuming splicing of tape. During their discussions they conceived of a "portable electronic music studio" that would be far more practical and sophisticated. Moog went on to apply for and secure a $16,000 grant to develop such an instrument. Earlier synthesisers which were the size of rooms used vacuum tubes to control the pitch and waveform of sounds. Moog's innovation was to use the latest silicon transistor technology such that voltage would control both sound and loudness. These VCO's (voltage controlled oscillators) and VCA's (voltage controlled amplifiers) were the heart of the Moog synthesiser. Moog demonstrated the new instrument in 1964 generating immediate interest due to its small size and low cost. A community of customers began experimenting with the Moog synthesiser which led to further enhancements. In 1970, Bob Moog released the Minimoog which has later been described as the most famous and influential synthesiser in history.

The Touch-Tone Telephone

Until 1963, the telephone worked on the principle of pulse dialling. The rotary dial mechanism would create a series of pulses corresponding to the number we put our finger in. Although robust as a signalling technology it was nonetheless slow! As early as the beginning of the 1940s, Western Electric had experimented with the design of push button telephones. However it wasn't until the invention of the transistor did such a system become a realistic possibility. It was the Bell System in the USA that first introduced dual-tone multi-frequency (DTMF) technology that allowed push button phones to become a reality. First

A Western Electric model 1500 from the 1960s

demonstrated publicly at the Seattle World's Fair in 1962, the system went live in 1963. Notably President John F. Kennedy started the countdown for the 1964 World's Fair by keying in "1964" on a touch-tone telephone in the Oval Office in April 1963. The digits are arranged in a grid on the phone. When a button is pressed it generates two tones of different frequencies; one indicating which row and the other indicating which column. The combination of these two (dual) tones identifies the specific key pressed. The distinct advantage of pulse dialling was the speed at which numbers could be dialled. Led by business users initially, DTMF dialling and push button phones became the global standard.

The Launch of the Compact Audio Cassette Tape

The Compact Audio Cassette

The origins of the audio cassette tape can be traced back to 1888 when American Oberlin Smith invented a method of recording sound by magnetising wire. This led to German Fritz Pfleumer inventing magnetic tape in 1928 which in turn led to the first reel-to-reel tape recorders appearing in 1935. However these machines were expensive and difficult to use, so were mostly found in radio stations and recording studios. It wasn't until 1963 when Lou Ottens and his team, working for Dutch company Phillips, commercially launched a miniaturised version of magnetic tape at the Berlin Radio Show. The compact audio cassette tape was born. It would go on to revolutionise how we listen to music. The ability to both take your music with you and also record your own 'mix tapes' caught the public's imagination. Although the development team initially envisaged the use of cassettes for dictation, the quality of the audio was such that its use for music quickly dominated. Sony turbocharged the demand for audio cassettes in 1979 when it released the first ever Walkman. The 3.81mm wide tape typically was made of polyester with a coating of Ferric Oxide which was magnetised to encode the recording. Two stereo pairs of tracks were available; one when the cassette was played in one direction and the other when the cassette was flipped, or in subsequent years, when an auto-reverse mechanism was actuated. The cassette tape remained the dominant music format until the 1990s when Compact Discs (CDs) arrived.

The Profumo Scandal

John Profumo's demise was summed up in a neat piece of doggerel: "To lie in the nude may be rude, but to lie in the House is obscene." The Profumo affair was a political scandal in 1963 in the UK that involved a British government minister, John Profumo, and a young woman named Christine Keeler. The scandal had a significant impact on the political landscape of the time and ultimately led to the fall of the Macmillan government. John Profumo was the Secretary of State for War. In the summer of 1961, he attended a party hosted by Lord Astor at his country house, Cliveden. It was there that Profumo met Christine Keeler, a 19-year-old aspiring model and showgirl. Keeler was also romantically involved with Yevgeny Ivanov, a Soviet naval

John Profumo

attaché, who was suspected of being a spy. Profumo and Keeler began an affair that lasted several months, but their relationship was exposed in March 1963 when Keeler's ex-boyfriend, Johnny Edgecombe, fired a gun at the door of her friend's house where Keeler was staying. This incident attracted media attention, and it was soon revealed that Keeler had also been involved with Ivanov. As the scandal unfolded, questions were raised about Profumo's relationship with Keeler and whether

Lord Astor's country mansion, Cliveden

he had compromised national security by passing on classified information to her or Ivanov. Profumo initially denied any wrongdoing and made a statement to the House of Commons in which he stated that there was no impropriety in his relationship with Keeler. However, as more information came to light, it became clear that Profumo had lied to Parliament. The scandal continued to escalate, and in June 1963, Profumo resigned from his position as Secretary of State for War and from Parliament. The scandal also eventually led to the resignation of the Prime Minister, Harold Macmillan, who was suffering from ill-health and faced criticism over his handling of the affair. The Conservative Party was badly damaged by the scandal losing the subsequent general election to the Labour Party. The Profumo affair became one of the most famous political scandals in British history and has been the subject of numerous books, films and TV dramas. It was seen as a symbol of the decline of the British establishment and a sign of the changing attitudes towards sex and

Christine Keeler

morality in the 1960s. The scandal also highlighted the dangers of mixing politics with personal relationships and the importance of maintaining the integrity of government institutions. The Profumo affair is frequently understood to mark a political watershed, the moment at which Macmillan's government became doomed. However, the popular culture that emerged from the scandal, with its willingness to mock and lacerate the political establishment, thus spoke to changing cultural and social values. The sixties of the Beatles and Carnaby Street suddenly made Macmillan, who had served in World War I, seem from a bygone age.

The Great Train Robbery

At around 3:00am on 8th August 1963, an armed gang boarded a Royal Mail train en route Glasgow to London. Dangerous and organised, they escaped with a staggering £2.3 million. Up until this time, Britain had a proud record of operating a vast rail network without a major robbery. Not only did the heist stun the nation because of the enormous amount of money stolen, it also captured their imagination as the highly organised style of the robbery seemed more like a movie script. Tales of a criminal gang coordinated by a single mastermind were soon spreading through the press. The mail train was stopped after the gang tampered with the railway signal at Cheddington by covering the green light with a glove and powering the red stop light with a battery. On stopping the train, the fireman walked to the nearest line-side

Bridego Bridge where the train was stopped. It was subsequently renamed Train Robber's Bridge after the heist.

telephone only to discover the wires had been cut. At this stage both he and the driver, Jack Mills, were brutally attacked. The injured driver was then forced to drive the train on to a pre-arranged meeting point, where the rest of the gang were waiting to unload the money. All the money was being transported in the HVP (High Value Packets) carriage which contained 4 postal workers and an assistant inspector, but crucially no police nor security staff. When one of the windows was smashed, one of the officers called out "It's a raid." The workers made a vain attempt to secure the carriage, but without security measures nor qualified staff they were outnumbered and soon overpowered. The 16-strong gang, led by mastermind Bruce Reynolds, formed a human chain and offloaded 120 out of the 128 mailbags full of cash in only 30 mins on to a waiting lorry. They drove back to a remote farm 27 miles away

Bruce Reynolds in 1999

where they had planned the heist. The money was divided up between the gang members totalling about £150,000 each (equivalent to £3million today). By monitoring police radio they realised the police were closing in faster then they had expected so they scattered the following day, two days earlier than planned. Most of the stolen money was never recovered, and if it wasn't for an informer giving names of the gang members to police, most of the assailants would have got away with it too. However with the names, the police were quick to catch up with the criminals with 11 being arrested and put on trial in January 1964. Most were given long sentences between 25 and 30 years. Bruce Reynolds and gang member Buster Edwards evaded capture ending up in Mexico City. In August 1964 another gang member, Charlie Wilson, successfully broke out of prison and managed to escape and meet up

Ronnie Biggs

with his colleagues in Mexico City. However, most famous for his prison escape and evasion of capture was minor gang member, Ronnie Biggs. He escaped from Wandsworth Prison in 1965, first fleeing to Paris where he had plastic surgery to disguise his appearance. He then fled to Melbourne, Australia and then on to Rio de Janeiro, Brazil where he lived openly until 2001 as Britain had no extradition treaty with Brazil. With failing health he then decided to voluntarily return to the UK where he was immediately arrested.

The Speeches of Martin Luther King Jr.

"I have a dream" the US civil rights leader Dr. Martin Luther King Jr. proclaimed to a crowd of over one quarter of a million from the steps of the Lincoln Memorial in Washington D.C. "I have a dream that my four children will one day live in a nation where they will not be judged by the colour of their skin but by the content of their character." On 28th August 1963, during the March on Washington for Jobs and Freedom, King delivered what is considered among the most important speeches in American history. Although the address totalled 17 minutes long, it is best remembered for its final few minutes, where King painted a picture of a unified America. In the wake of the speech and march, President John F. Kennedy and his administration were put under pressure to advance civil rights legislation in Congress. On 3rd April 1968 King delivered his "I Have Been to the Mountain

Martin Luther King Jr. giving the "I have a dream" speech

Top" speech in which he declared "Because I've been to the mountaintop ..... Like anybody, I would like to live a long life. Longevity has its place, but I'm not concerned about that now. I just want to do God's will, and he's allowed me to go up to the mountain. And I've looked over, and I've seen the promised land. I may not get there with you, but I want you to know tonight, that we as a people, will get to the promised land." King's prophetic words rang true. He was assassinated by James Earl Ray just one day later. Martin Luther King Jr. Day was signed into US federal law in 1983 and took effect three years later. The holiday takes place on the third Monday of January each year and commemorates the life and work of the Baptist minister and activist.

250,000 attended the speech

On the March on Washington for Jobs and Freedom

The speech has been hailed as the greatest of all time

Haile Selassie Addresses the United Nations

On 4th October 1963, Haile Selassie I returned to appear before the plenary session of the United Nations, just as he did in 1936 when he was the first Head of State to stand in front of that podium alerting Europe to the threat of Italian fascism. In this speech, the emperor of Ethiopia again called for world peace and the end to racial discrimination: "Until the philosophy that sustains a superior and inferior race is finally and permanently discredited and abandoned; until there are no first and second class citizens of any nation; until the colour of a man's skin is no more important than the colour of his eyes; until basic human rights are equally guaranteed to all regardless of race; that until that day, the dream of lasting peace and world citizenship and the rule of international morality, will remain a fleeting illusion, hunted but never reached. And until the ignoble and unhappy regimes that keep our brothers in Angola, in Mozambique and South Africa in subhuman servitude have been shot down, destroyed. Until intolerance and prejudice and malicious and inhuman selfishness have

Haile Selassie I in 1963

been replaced by understanding, tolerance and goodwill. Until all Africans stand up and speak like free human beings, equal in the eyes of all men, as they are in the eyes of heaven; until that day, the African continent will not know peace."

Ich bin ein Berliner | 26th June 1963

The US President, John F. Kennedy, made a ground-breaking speech in Berlin offering American solidarity to the citizens of West Germany. A crowd of 120,000 Berliners gathered in front of the Schöneberg Rathaus (City Hall) to hear President Kennedy speak. They began gathering in the square long before he was due to arrive, and when he finally appeared on the podium they gave him an ovation of several minutes. The president had just returned from a visit on foot to one of the Berlin Wall's most notorious crossing points, Checkpoint Charlie. He was watched from the other side of the border by small groups of East Berliners unable even to wave because of the presence of large groups of the East German People's Police. In an impassioned speech, the president told them West Berlin was a symbol of freedom in a world threatened by the Cold War. "Two thousand years ago," he told the crowd, "the proudest boast in the world was 'civis Romanus sum'." Today, in the world of freedom, the proudest boast is 'Ich bin

JFK in front of the crowd

ein Berliner. Freedom has many difficulties and democracy is not perfect," he continued "but we never had to put up a wall to keep our people in." He ended on the theme he had begun with: "All free men, wherever they may live, are citizens of Berlin, and therefore, as a free man, I take pride in the words, 'Ich bin ein Berliner.'"

The Beeching Cuts

"Oh, Dr. Beeching what have you done? There once were lots of trains to catch, but soon there will be none, I'll have to buy a bike, 'cos I can't afford a car, Oh, Dr. Beeching what a naughty man you are!"

Dr. Richard Beeching was recruited by the government from a very successful business career at ICI to make the railways profitable again. On 27th March 1963, he published his report entitled 'The Reshaping of British Railways." By the early 1960s the industry was losing millions of pounds a year. His solution was simple: close down the bits that lost the money. The Beeching report recommended taking an axe to about a third of the network - 5,000 miles of track, including hundreds of branch lines, 2,363 stations and tens of thousands of jobs. Instead, it would concentrate on the things trains did well: fast journeys between the cities. Improved bus services could replace branch lines, argued Dr. Beeching. In a public information film at the time he said: "On one half of the whole route mileage of British Railways, there is only one 20th of the traffic... the real question is whether you, as owners of the railways, want us to go on running these services at very high cost when the demand for them has very largely disappeared." The report was explosive. Railway enthusiast and ex-Monty Python star Michael Palin was asked his opinion on Beeching. He replied "(He was) definitely a villain, to me, but then I always have been a huge supporter of railways. There was something about the scale and the brutality of the attack that I remember at

Dr. Beeching and his infamous report

the time made me feel that this is wrong." His memories echo so many others from the time, as the Beeching axe left its mark across Britain. Palin continued: "The line through from Sheffield to Manchester where we lived and grew up, which had the great Woodhead tunnel, one of the longest tunnels in the world, three miles long, the tunnel was closed while they built a motorway over the Pennines. It had very profound effects in our city." Interestingly there were some branch lines which were kept open. Mainly the ones that passed through marginal constituencies, such as those in South

Prospect Tunnel on the Harrogate to Church Fenton line was one of the first lines to close under the cuts

and Mid-Wales. The Conservative government of the day may have had one eye on the balance sheet, but they also had another on the ballot box. Two branch lines running from London to Essex and Suffolk were also kept open. These linked the network to the Nuclear power stations at Bradwell and Sizewell. As it was considered unsafe to transport radioactive materials by road the railway was kept open. It is also possible to travel by rail to Seascale near Calder Hall, then Windscale, in Cumbria, the UK's first nuclear plant. Others like Private Eye editor Ian Hislop think that Beeching was unfairly judged. After all he was a civil servant, charged with delivering a report and it fell to the government of the day to implement it. Beeching also called for a large expansion of the UK's bus network to compensate for the closure of railway lines. Successive administrations failed to deliver on this promise.

The Winter of 1962/63

The Big Freeze of 1962-63 was one of the coldest winters on record in the UK. When we look at the Central England Temperature records, which extend back to 1659, only the winters of 1683-84 and 1739-40 have been colder. The most severe conditions were across England and Wales. Although winter hit hard in Scotland, it didn't rank as one of its worst on record. The temperatures plummeted for weeks on end causing rivers, lakes and even the sea to freeze over. The first few weeks of December 1962 had been changeable and stormy, but then on 22nd December there was a sudden change in the weather as high pressure moved to the north-east of the UK dragging bitingly cold winds across the country. Once this weather pattern had set in, it did not change much

Telephone wires collapsed under the ice

for the rest of the winter. On 24th December a weather front moved south across the UK turning to snow as it did so. Glasgow had its first white Christmas since 1938. The snow reached southern England on Boxing Day with some places seeing falls of up to 12 inches. A blizzard on 29th and 30th December hit Wales and the south west of England causing snowdrifts up to 20ft deep. Widespread disruption followed as many roads and railways were blocked and telephone lines brought down leaving some villages left cut off for several days. Poole Harbour froze over, as did a section of the Thames in Berkshire. The snow was so deep that farmers couldn't get to their livestock causing many animals to perish. On Dartmoor, 6,000 animals went without food for 4 days until helicopters could drop in supplies. The effect on wildlife was also severe. The New Forest's Dartford warbler

Deep snow in Lancashire

population was almost wiped out. Garden birds such as the wren and the goldcrest saw their numbers greatly depleted. This snow set the scene for the next two and a half months, as much of England remained covered every day until early March 1963. Blizzards, snowdrifts and blocks of ice were commonplace with temperatures dropping below -20°C, colder than the winter of 1947 and the coldest since 1740. In Braemar, Scotland, the temperature plummeted to -22.2°C on 18th January. Sport suffered greatly and the 3rd round of the F.A. Cup took 66 days to complete. Manchester City went 70 days without playing a match. When football could be played it took place on icy pitches. On 26th December 1962, Brian Clough suffered a career ending injury

Clearing this drive took all day

caused by a slippery pitch. Although he made a short-lived comeback two years later, he then retired and became the greatest manager of his generation. The thaw didn't truly begin until the beginning of March 1963 when mild, south westerly winds led to an increase in the temperature. By 6th March, there were no frosts anywhere in the UK and the temperature in London reached 17°C. The snow quickly melted and with the thaw came flooding, though thankfully none of it was major.

Exposing Government Secrets

On the afternoon of 16th February 1963 four men set out from London for an area of countryside just outside Reading in Berkshire. All were members of a British anti-nuclear direct action group known as the Committee of 100. What they eventually came across, and gained access to, was Regional Seat of Government 6 (RSG6). This was one of a network of nuclear bunkers from which an elite were to govern the country in the event of a nuclear attack. Following a second visit, a suitcase of sensitive material was given to a wider group for collective analysis.

The former RSG6 at the University of Reading

This small group of activists, under the name 'Spies for Peace', then secretly collated the procured information and produced the controversial document *Danger! Official Secret*. On 10th April, 3,000 copies were sent out to carefully chosen members of the public in time for widespread copying and distribution on the Easter Aldermaston march. The march coincidentally passed within a few miles of RSG6 and on the Saturday, a section of the marchers split from the organised route and headed towards the government installation, where they protested outside the entrance for a few hours. Media outcry ensued and for the British public a crisis in confidence in their political leadership. Despite parliamentary pressure on the authorities to pursue those responsible, none of the spies was ever caught for their actions. The pamphlet explained what they had discovered about the regional seats of government that would spring into action in the event of nuclear war. They duplicated 3,000 copies of the pamphlet, destroying the originals, even throwing the typewriter they had used into a canal. They posted them to members of the peace movement, plus journalists, celebrities and MPs. Those optimistic days of protest and song were not all for nothing. The Spies for Peace did not, as they hoped, usher in an age of nuclear disarmament and government openness. But their influence did not begin and end in April 1963. These days, the idea of government hatching a baroque and secretive system for surviving nuclear war would be seen as the delusional folly it is. The Spies were part of the much wider movement of liberalisation which

Inside The Barnton Quarry Bunker, Edinburgh. It was also designated a Regional Seat of Government in the 1960s

came to characterise the 1960s, the time that transformed a grey and deferential Britain into something much more colourful and questioning. It was not until after their deaths that the identities of some of the spies were revealed. The list includes anarchists Ruth and Nicholas Walker. It was also revealed posthumously that mathematical philosopher Mike Lesser was part of the group. The actions of the "Spies for Peace" divided opinion. To some they were heroes of a peaceful protest movement akin to those of Dr. Martin Luther King Jr. and Mahatma Gandhi. To others, they were treasonous criminals no better than spies like Kim Philby of the Cambridge Spy Ring.

Kim Philby and The Cambridge Spies

Kim Philby was a high-ranking British intelligence officer who, along with a group of fellow Cambridge-educated spies, passed sensitive information to the Soviet Union during the Cold War. He was a member of the infamous Cambridge Spy Ring, which also included Donald Maclean, Guy Burgess, Anthony Blunt and perhaps John Cairncross. The spy ring was formed in the 1930s when its members were students at Cambridge University. They were all members of the Communist Party or sympathetic to its cause. In the early days of World War II, the group offered their services to the Soviet Union and began to pass on classified information. Philby, who was recruited by Soviet intelligence in the 1930s, joined the British Secret Intelligence Service (SIS), which later became known as MI6, in 1940. He quickly rose through the ranks and by the 1950s was one of the agency's top officers. During this time, he had access to some of the UK's most sensitive intelligence, including information on atomic weapons and counter-intelligence operations. However, Philby's allegiance to the Soviet Union was uncovered in

Double Agent Kim Philby

1963 when a Soviet defector revealed that he was a spy. He was forced to flee to the Soviet Union, where he spent the rest of his life. In 1979, he was awarded the Order of Lenin by the Soviet Union for his services to the country. The Cambridge Spy Ring was one of the most successful espionage collectives in history and it is estimated that they passed on thousands of secret documents to the Soviet Union. The information they provided gave the Soviet Union a significant advantage in the early days of the Cold War. The discovery of the spy ring had a profound impact on British intelligence and led to a major reorganisation of the country's intelligence services. It also damaged the reputation of the British establishment and raised questions about how such a group of individuals could have infiltrated the highest levels of government and intelligence. The Cambridge Spy Ring and its members have been the subject of numerous books, films and TV shows. The fate of the other spies was mixed. Maclean fled to Russia to be lauded as a hero. Blunt worked for MI5 during the war. After the war he had a distinguished career as an art historian.

The Order of Lenin medal

He was director of the Courtauld Institute and Surveyor of the Queen's Pictures. He was knighted in 1956. In 1963, the British government discovered he was a spy but offered him immunity in return for information. In 1979, the story got out and Blunt was stripped of his knighthood. Guy Burgess, who defected to the Soviet Union in 1951, died on 30th August 1963 aged 52. The playwright Alan Bennett saw things differently from the established view when he wrote in 1991 "No one has ever shown that Burgess did much harm, except to make fools of people in high places." Philby died in Moscow in 1988. He was given a hero's funeral and posthumously awarded numerous medals by the Soviets.

Tottenham Hotspur | The Heroes of Rotterdam

Tottenham Hotspur's starting lineup

Bill Nicholson's side thrashed Atlético Madrid 5-1 in the final of the European Cup Winners' Cup in Rotterdam. Tottenham's success came after a string of near misses for the UK. Manchester United had twice lost in the European Cup semi-finals, the second time weeks after the Munich air disaster. Hibernian, Rangers, Dundee and Spurs had also previously reached the last four – with Tottenham losing to eventual winners Benfica in 1962. The Cup Winners' Cup was in its third season with Rangers having lost to Fiorentina in the first final while the Inter-Cities Fairs Cup, the precursor to the UEFA Cup, had seen a London XI and Birmingham City twice losing in finals. Spurs qualified for the tournament when they retained the FA Cup with a 3-1 Wembley win over Burnley. Their run started with an emphatic win over Rangers, beating them home and away in an 8-4 aggregate victory before overturning a 2-0 first-leg deficit with a 6-0 thrashing of Slovan Bratislava at White Hart Lane. Spurs then reached the final by beating Yugoslavian cup winners OFK Beograd 5-2 on aggregate. In the final, Jimmy Greaves and Terry Dyson both hit doubles as Spurs romped to victory. Greaves opened the scoring with a brilliant first-time finish before Scotland international John White fired high into the net. Atlético pulled one back from the spot just after the interval and Spurs had some nervy moments before the Spanish side's goalkeeper let Dyson's cross slip through his hands and into the net. Greaves and Dyson added to the scoreline with expertly-taken strikes. The triumph continued a trophy-laden spell in the history of Tottenham, following on from their double in 1961 and retaining the FA Cup the following season. Spurs finished runners-up in the league in the season of their European triumph, during a run when they were in the top three in six seasons out of seven. Nicholson's side had also won the Charity Shield in 1961 and 1962 and went on to win the FA Cup in 1967. After football, the career paths of the team went in different directions. Northern Ireland born captain, Blanchflower, was seen as a successor to the manager Bill Nicholson, but when Nicholson retired in 1974, his was passed over in favour of Terry Neill. Jimmy Greaves, one of England's greatest strikers, went on to find fame as a pundit on the football show *Saint And Greavsie*, with Liverpool stalwart Ian St. John. But for most of the team they had to re-qualify and take other jobs, there was simply not enough money in football to allow them a comfortable retirement. Right back Peter Barker emigrated to Durban, South Africa, where he set up a stationery business; left back Ron Henry bought a plot of land which he converted into a plant nursery and also reared homing pigeons. Terry Dyson gained a teaching qualification and became a much loved PE teacher at Hampstead School in London.

The Wimbledon Lawn Tennis Championships 1963

Chuck McKinley posing for photos after his victory

Few people could entertain on a grass court quite like the ebullient American Charles "Chuck" McKinley. An all-action player who loved to attack, he threw himself to all corners of the court, dived to hit volleys that were seemingly beyond his reach and chased down his opponents' shots as if his life depended on it. No wonder that crowds around the world loved him. He recognised a kindred spirit when 17-year-old Boris Becker won the Gentlemen's Singles title at The Championships in similar fashion, 22 years after his own triumph. Although he was one of the last amateur champions, McKinley's background was by no means privileged. Born in Dallas, Texas, he grew up in a blue-collar environment in St. Louis where he excelled at tennis, table tennis, baseball and basketball. He learned to play tennis at St. Louis YMCA, a teacher having encouraged him to take up the sport after recognising his talent on the table tennis table. Although only 5ft 8in tall, short by tennis standards, he was a fine all-round athlete who was quick, strong and with apparently bottomless reserves of energy. In 1963, McKinley proved unstoppable as he won the All England Club title in hugely impressive fashion. Cliff Drysdale and Arthur Ashe were among his early victims. He also beat Britain's Bobby Wilson in the quarter-finals for the second time in three years. A 6-2, 6-4, 8-6 victory over Wilhelm Bungert put McKinley through to the final, in which he beat Australia's Fred Stolle 9-7, 6-1, 6-4. He is one of only five men alongside Don Budge (1938), Tony Trabert (1955), Bjorn Borg (1976) and Roger Federer (2017) who have won the gentlemen's singles title at Wimbledon without dropping a set.

Although McKinley returned to defend his title the following year, he found progress much more difficult. Thomaz Koch took him to five sets in the second round, while Torben Ullrich, Billy Knight and Abe Segal each took a set off the American before he met Stolle in the semi-finals. McKinley won the first set, but the Australian recovered to win 4-6, 10-8, 9-7, 6-4. Stolle reached three successive finals but lost all of them, to McKinley in 1963 and to Roy Emerson in 1964 and 1965. McKinley played his last match at Wimbledon in 1964 where he lost in the semi-final in four sets to Fred Stolle. He never played at the Australian or French Opens but made 11 appearances in singles at his home Grand Slam event, the US National Tennis Championships. Here he reached the semi-finals three times. He won three doubles titles in New York, partnering Dennis Ralston to victory in 1961, 1963 and 1964.

Rugby Union

New Zealand embarked upon a four-month tour of the British Isles, France and Canada. A hugely powerful and skilled side containing the likes of All Black greats Colin Meads and Don Clarke were to play 36 games and lose just one, with Newport RFC in Wales the team to claim the most famous win in their history. Wilson Whinneray's 1963 All Blacks arrived in the northern hemisphere towards the end of October warming up with a 19-3 win over Oxford University, before thrashing Southern Counties 32-3 in Hove. On 30th October the Kiwis arrived at a wet Rodney Parade in Newport to face a Black and Ambers side whose early season form gave little indication that they would provide much of a contest for one of the finest touring sides in New Zealand history. Newport had managed just 6 wins and 2 draws from their opening 12 matches, but the Welsh side's 13th fixture was to prove unlucky for New Zealand. Compared to the star-studded tourists, Newport's starting XV contained just five players with international experience. But

Wilson Whinneray

the Black and Ambers had leadership in abundance, with captain Brian Price and vice-captain David Watkins fulfilling that role for both their club and for Wales that season. "We weren't very worried about it before the game and I suppose we took them too lightly," admitted All Black Meads. "We found out you don't take any Welsh clubs lightly when they're playing the All Blacks." As it happened, just one score was enough to win the contest 3-0 and it came 17 minutes into the game. New Zealand would not lose another game on the '63 tour, although Scotland would hold them 0-0 at Murrayfield. This underlined Newport's achievement, creating a golden moment that would enter South Wales' rugby folklore.

Rugby League

Swinton won the Lancashire Cup in dramatic style against Widnes in 1940, but thereafter the War curtailed the promise of further progress. By the time Britain emerged from the storm clouds Swinton had lost their way. Throughout the 1940s and 1950s the Swinton Lions strove unsuccessfully to repeat former glories and often flattered to deceive. However, the appointment of Welshman Cliff Evans as coach signalled a renaissance. Concentrating on a youth policy and training methods beyond his era, Evans began to model an exciting, young Swinton team. It all came to fruition in 1963 when, under the shrewd captaincy of Albert Blan, the Lions completed the final 18 games of a 30 match league calendar undefeated to walk away with the Championship. To complete two remarkable seasons, Swinton's 6th title was retained in style 12 months later. The Lions' backline of the early 60s still rolls off the tongues of those who witnessed them in full flow.

Swinton's home ground in 1963

Ken Gowers, John Speed, Bobby Fleet, Alan Buckley, Johnny Stopford, George Parkinson and Graham Williams. Even in an era where the unlimited tackle rule ensured much tighter matches, these players could create a try from any position on the field.

The Arrival of the Windies | Pace like fire, but spin too

The West Indies' Touring Team of 1963

At the first Test, England faced up to the feared fast bowling partnership of Charlie Griffith and Wes Hall, but it was off-spinner Lance Gibbs who proved hardest to handle in a 10-wicket defeat at Old Trafford. Conrad Hunte's 182, supported by 90 from Rohan Kanhai, led West Indies to 501 for six declared. Although skipper Ted Dexter made 73, England were all out for 205 with Gibbs taking five for 59. Micky Stewart, father of future England wicket-keeper and skipper Alec, scored 87 as the home side followed on but no-one else reached fifty as Gibbs surpassed his first innings display with figures of six for 98. England were dismissed for 296 and Hunte collected the single needed for victory. England recalled Derek Shackleton for a thrilling second Test at Lord's where he picked up seven wickets in a drawn game, providing an ideal foil for the pace of Fred Trueman who returned match figures of 11 for 152. The tourists totalled 301 batting first but England finished only four runs adrift thanks to 80 by Ken Barrington and 70 from Dexter, who shared a third wicket stand of 82. Basil Butcher's 133 was more than half of West Indies' second innings 229, which left England 234 to win. Barrington's 60 and a typically defiant 70 from Brian Close gave them a chance but the tourists chipped their way through the order and the match ended with England on 228 for nine and so was drawn.

Trueman produced another dynamic display at Edgbaston, where England levelled the series with a 217 run win. England's total of 216 did not look good enough after winning the toss, but Trueman snapped up five for 75, supported well by Dexter's four for 38, to leave West Indies 30 runs behind on first innings. Phil Sharpe's determined 85 not out in his first Test appearance enabled England to declare on 278 for 9 early on the fifth day and Trueman ripped through the middle order for figures of 7 for 44 as West Indies collapsed to 91 all out. In the fourth test at Headingly, Sobers starred with the bat and paceman Griffiths with the ball as the West Indies ran out comfortable winners. A hard-fought series came to an end at The Oval with West Indies coming out on top by a 3-1 margin thanks to a 221-run win. Gary Sobers (102) and Kanhai (92) guided the tourists to 397 after they won the toss and Griffith was in destructive mood as he took 6 for 36 as England were hustled out for 174. England's bowlers performed well to restrict West Indies to 229 in their second innings with off-spinner Fred Titmus claiming 4 for 44, but the task of scoring 453 for victory was beyond them. Half centuries by Brian Close and Jim Parks were little consolation as they were dismissed for 231.

When A Great Met The Greatest

When Mill House lined up, as a six-year-old, for his first attempt in the Cheltenham Gold Cup in 1963, he was hailed as the best horse in Britain, a once in a generation chaser. Owned by Bill Gollings and trained by Fulke Walwyn, he was referred to as 'The Big Horse' on account of his near-seventeen hand height. Mill House, was at this stage, considered unbeatable. He was compared with multiple Gold Cup winners Golden Miller, who won 5 Gold Cups in the 1930s and Easter Hero, who won two on the bounce in 1929-30. Competition for Mill House in the 1963 Cheltenham Gold Cup came from the Tom Dreaper trained Fortria, who had finished second in the

Arkle (left) and Mill House (right) in one of their epic encounters

race a year earlier. Fortria was expected to pose a threat, but the projected duel failed to materialise. Ridden by his regular partner, Willie Robinson, Mill House travelled and jumped imperiously throughout and, as soon as he was given his head turning for home, it became clear that, barring accidents, the race was all over bar the shouting. Another flying leap at the final fence put the result beyond any doubt and the towering bay gelding galloped home in splendid isolation, to rapturous applause from the home contingent. Fortria and Duke Of York both stayed on gamely in the closing stages, but there was no catching Mill House, who eventually beat Fortria by 12 lengths with Duke Of York a further 4 lengths away in third place.

While every sport needs its greats, like Jack Nicklaus in golf or Muhammad Ali in boxing, it also needs great rivalries. Nicklaus had Tom Watson and Ali had Frazier. Something was brewing in Ireland that would change the face of jumps racing forever. A five-year-old named Arkle won two hurdle races in Ireland before being sent over to Cheltenham, where he won the Honeybourne Chase. In March 1963, Arkle made his Cheltenham Festival debut, winning the Broadway Novice Chase by 12 lengths. Arkle's first encounter with Mill House was in the 1963 Hennessey Gold Cup and it was first blood to Mill House after Arkle made a bad error at the third last. Thereafter, it was Arkle all the way with the gelding dominating steeplechase racing. He won the Cheltenham Gold Cup three times (1964-66), the Irish Grand National (1964) as well as three Leopardstown Gold Cups (1964-6). He finished his career in 1967 with a win record of 27 from 34 starts. He was also given a Timeform rating (the definitive assessment of the merit of a racehorse's form) of 212, which will never be equalled. Mill House was given a rating of 191 making him the joint fourth rated chaser of all time, meaning that even if Arkle conceded 18lbs to Mill House in a handicap, he would still have won.

Ford Vs Ferrari

In 1963, the story of the World Sports Car Championship was one of Ferrari's dominance with its mighty 250 GTO. By the tenth round, the annual running of the 24 Hours of Le Mans, it was clear nothing could touch them. In fact, Ferraris finished the race in the top six places. The experimental Rover-BRM Turbine of Graham Hill and Richie Ginther which managed 310 laps ran well enough to finish in seventh place. The American giant Ford was nowhere to be seen. In the early 1960s, Henry Ford II's love for car racing was part of the reason that he decided that the Ford Motor Company would start competing. The other part had to do with the fact that Ford needed a marketing boost in the face of slipping sales and stiff competition from General Motors especially when it came to attracting younger buyers. The only problem was that Ford didn't have a sports racing car in its fleet. By 1963, Henry Ford II (the grandson and namesake of the company's founder) decided that the quickest way to get Ford on the racetrack would be to buy Ferrari. Ford sent a group of dealmakers to Modena, Italy to hash out a deal with Enzo Ferrari who himself was an accomplished

Ferrari's all conquering 250 GTO pictured in 1963

driver. Months of meticulous negotiation followed. At first, Enzo agreed to the deal, but there was a clause in the contract which stated that Ford would control the racing budget and in turn all decisions. Enzo Ferrari (also known as "Il Commendatore") couldn't handle the idea that anyone else would control the decisions regarding his race team, so he defaulted on the deal. It even got personal with Enzo Ferrari telling Henry Ford II that he was only a fraction of a man that his grandfather was. There is a popular belief that Ferrari used Ford to leverage a better deal from eventual buyers Fiat. But Fiat did not buy a stake in Ferrari until 1969. Spurred on by Ferrari's snub and the insults from its owner, Ford redoubled efforts to produce a car that would challenge for motorsport's premier event. This paid off in 1966 when a Ford GT 40 Mk. II driven by New Zealanders Chris Amon and Bruce McLaren took the "24." Ford would dominate the race until 1969 when Brit Jackie Oliver and Belgian Jacky Ickx won. Bruce McLaren's name

Ford's GT40 would dominate in the latter half of the 1960's

would endure. He was not only a great driver, but also a genius innovator and inventor. Although he died, aged just 32, when his Can-Am car crashed on the Lavant Straight, just before Woodcote Corner at Goodwood racetrack on 2nd June 1970, his name would live on via the highly successful eponymous Formula One racing team. The story of Ford and Ferrari was turned into a movie in 2019. The film *Ford v Ferrari* (also called Le Mans 66), starred Matt Damon as Carroll Shelby and Christian Bale as British driver Ken Miles.

Henry Cooper versus Cassius Clay

Wembley Stadium, London
18th June 1963

Henry Cooper, popularly known as 'Our 'Enry', was one of the most celebrated and successful British boxers of all time. Cooper turned professional at the age of 20 in 1954 and went on to enjoy a highly successful professional career. Although he never won a world title, he was British and Commonwealth heavyweight champion between 1959 and 1971 and European heavyweight champion between 1968 and 1971. However, for all his success, Cooper is probably best remembered for his narrow and controversial defeat by 21-year-old Cassius Clay (soon to change his name to Muhammad Ali) in a non-title fight at Wembley Stadium, London in June 1963. The match very nearly changed the course of boxing history. Before the fight, Clay had brashly predicted, "It ain't no jive, Henry Cooper will go in five!" He also lived up to his nickname the "Louisville Lip" when he described Cooper as "a tramp, a bum, and a cripple not worth training for." Cooper, ever the gentleman, took it in good heart stating "Let him carry on. I'm on the gate, he's selling tickets and earning me good money." Nevertheless, towards the end of the fourth round, Cooper 28, unleashed a trademark left hook, dubbed "Enry's 'Ammer', which knocked Clay to the canvas for a count of four. When the bell sounded, Clay was sitting on the seat of his pants, back

Henry Cooper was defeated by Cassius Clay by technical knockout

against the ropes and had to be walked back to his stool by trainer Angelo Dundee. Dundee administered smelling salts, which was against the rules and if the referee had noticed it would have resulted in Clay's disqualification. Dundee then spotted a split in Clay's glove, which he brought to the attention of the referee Tommy Little. According to Cooper, Dundee subsequently freely admitted, more than once, that he had deliberately slashed the glove to give Clay more time to recover between rounds. A replacement pair of gloves was fetched from the dressing room and, in the fifth round, a rejuvenated Clay set to work on slicing up Cooper's already bloodied face. A heavily bleeding cut over his left eye left Cooper unable to see properly and the contest was stopped. Clay won by technical knockout. There were claims that the torn glove gave Clay four minutes to recover, but study of the video of the fight shows that the break between rounds was a mere six seconds above the minute.

The two would meet again at Arsenal's Stadium in 1966. By this time, Clay had changed his name to Muhammad Ali. This time, Ali had learned his lesson and allowed Cooper no room to land his famous 'ammer. Again cuts to the face hampered Cooper and the fight was stopped in the fourth round.

Golf

The Open | Royal Lytham & St. Annes, England | 10th to 13th July 1963

Bob Charles put on one of the finest ever displays of putting in winning The Open at Royal Lytham & St. Annes. In so doing he became the first New Zealander and the first left-hander to win The Open. It would take another 50 years before another left-hander, Phil Mickelson, won at Muirfield in 2013. Charles claimed his victory in the last ever 36-hole play-off, beating American Phil Rodgers by eight strokes. The pair had tied on 277 after Charles had posted a best-of-the-week 66 in the third round to lead by two but Rodgers caught him with a closing 69. Jack Nicklaus, in his second Open, made a rare error at the final hole. His bogey left him one stroke outside the play-off. The play-off protagonists made a contrasting pair, Charles, tall and thin as a rake, was a quiet and undemonstrative man. Rodgers was a short, solidly-built ex-Marine who had a habit of racing across the green and slamming his cap over the hole when a long

Bob Charles

putt dropped. Most of the putts dropped for Charles. He made 11 single-putts in the morning round of the play-off. Seven times he got up and down from rough or bunkers. Three ahead at lunch and soon five in front, Charles hooked out of bounds onto the railway line at the third in the afternoon and then Rodgers made a couple of birdies to get within one. But his second at the seventh finished under the face of a greenside bunker and his challenge faded. Charles relentlessly kept holing putts to pull away again. In his rounds of 69-71 Charles had 56 putts. Rodgers totalled 65 putts in rounds of 72-76. It was Bob Charles' only ever major win. Rodgers' second place finish was the best he ever achieved, but the man in third place, Jack Nicklaus, finished his career with 18 major titles, a total that is unlikely to be beaten.

The Natal Open | Durban Country Club, South Africa

Sewsunker Sewgolum (aged 34) was an impoverished caddie who grew up in a tin shack not far from the Durban course; he never went to school and could neither read nor write. In 1963, he was given permission to compete in the Natal Open, a tournament that had previously refused his presence because of the colour of his skin. Playing the game with his characteristic serenity and a strange upside-down grip, the man they called "Papwa," who had never had a golf lesson in his life, overcame some of the best South African professionals of the day to win the tournament. It was an astonishing victory. To the large Indian community in Durban and to observers around the world, Papwa was a revelation, a homespun hero, a dark-skinned David in a world of white golfing Goliaths. What happened next became known as "the prize-giving that shook the world." Because it was raining, the

"Papwa" Sewgolum on the tee

logical place for the ceremony was inside the clubhouse. But in the apartheid system, Papwa was categorised as "non-white"; the sanctuary of the clubhouse was exclusively for whites. The champion was therefore hurriedly handed the trophy outside.

The iconic Aston Martin DB5 was launched in 1963. It was designed by the Italian coachbuilding company Carrozzeria Touring Superleggera. Most famously, it appeared in the 1964 film Goldfinger as 007's gadget-laden car. The DB in DB5 stands for David Brown, who led the company since 1947.

The Mercedes-Benz W113 was a 2-seater roadster and coupé launched at the 1963 Geneva Motor Show. It was available with 3 engine sizes, hence being known as either the 230 SL, 250 SL or 280 SL. The hardtop version earned the nickname "Pagoda" due to its unusual concave design. The car was in production until 1971 with nearly 50,000 examples sold.

First flown in August 1963, the Lockheed YF-12 was a high-altitude interceptor prototype capable of Mach 3+ developed and constructed by the American aerospace manufacturer Lockheed Corporation. It was very similar to the then-secret Lockheed A-12 used for reconnaissance by the CIA.

The first ever Learjet took to the skies on the 7th October 1963. The Lear Jet 23 was a twin jet, high speed airplane designed by American inventor and businessman William Powell Lear. This first model had 6 to 8 seats accommodating 4 to 6 passengers and 2 crew. The brand soon became an aspirational symbol synonymous with executive, luxury travel.

The Lava lamp was invented by British accountant Edward Craven Walker. His inspiration came whilst in the pub when he saw a homemade egg timer consisting of a cocktail shaker filled with strange liquids bubbling on a stove.

The Kodak Instamatic 50, a simple snapshot camera, was launched in the UK in February 1963. The Instamatic 100 model which included a built-in flash was launched in the US one month later for $16.

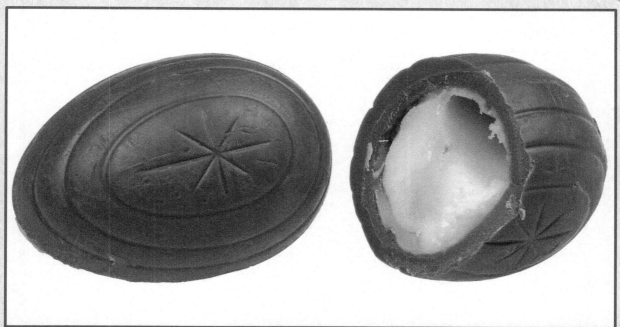

The Fry's Creme Egg, which was renamed in 1971 as the Cadbury's Creme Egg, was introduced in 1963. The sweet fondant filling is made to mimic the white albumen and yellow yolk of a soft boiled egg.

The Swedish packaging company AB Tetra Pak first introduced their rectangular Tetra Brik packaging in 1963. Available with or without caps this iconic design was based on the company's original tetrahedron (triangular) packaging.

Photo Credits

Credits shown in the order in which they appear in the book. Photos not listed are in the public domain.

Key to page numbers

fc = front cover; **tp** = title page; **cp** = contents page; **ap1** = acknowledgements page 1; **ap2** = acknowledgements page 2; **rop** = reader offer page; **ibc** = inside back cover; **bc** = back cover; **3** = page 3; **4** = page 4; etc.

Key to object position on page

tl = top left; *t* = top; *tc* = top centre; *tr* = top right; *cla* = centre left above; *ca* = centre above; *cra* = centre right above; *cl* = centre left; *c* = centre; *cr* = centre right; *clb* = centre left below; *cb* = centre below; *crb* = centre right below; *bl* = bottom left; *b* = bottom; *bc* = bottom centre; *br* = bottom right; *w* = whole page; *h* = header; *tb* = text background

Key to image licence types

CC BY-SA 2.0 = https://creativecommons.org/licenses/by-sa/2.0/deed.en;
CC BY-SA 3.0 = https://creativecommons.org/licenses/by-sa/3.0/deed.en;
CC BY-SA 4.0 = https://creativecommons.org/licenses/by-sa/4.0/deed.en;
(m) = image has been modified as permitted under licensing terms

fc *cla*: Queen Elizabeth II (m) © Archives New Zealand, Wikimedia Commons, CC BY-SA 2.0; **fc** *cra*: Duke of Edinburgh (m) © Archives New Zealand, Wikimedia Commons, CC BY-SA 2.0; **fc** *clb*: Paul McCartney (m) © Marcus, Wikimedia Commons, CC BY-SA 4.0; **tp** *w*: Aston Martin DB5 (m) © Daniel / Adobe Stock; **3** *tc*: The Beatles (m) © West Midlands Police, Wikimedia Commons, CC BY-SA 2.0; **18** *cla*: José Mourinho © Дмитрий Голубович, Wikimedia Commons, CC BY-SA 3.0; **19** *cla*: Seal © Eva Rinaldi , Wikimedia Commons, CC BY-SA 2.0; **19** *clb*: Quentin Tarantino © Gage Skidmore, Wikimedia Commons, CC BY-SA 3.0; **20** *cla*: Graham Norton © Raph_PH, Wikimedia Commons, CC BY-SA 3.0; **20** *clb*: Garry Kasparov © Fryta 73 from Strzegom, Wikimedia Commons, CC BY-SA 2.0; **21** *cla*: Natasha Richardson © bucksboy, Wikimedia Commons, CC BY-SA 2.0; **21** *clb*: Johnny Depp © Arnold Wells / Johnny Depp, Wikimedia Commons, CC BY-SA 2.0; **22** *cla*: George Michael © Sodel Vladyslav on Shutterstock.com; **22** *clb*: Tracey Emin © Piers Allardyce, Wikimedia Commons, CC BY-SA 2.0; **23** *cla*: Mark Strong © Gage Skidmore, Wikimedia Commons, CC BY-SA 3.0; **23** *clb*: Whitney Houston © John Mathew Smith & www.celebrity-photos.com, Wikimedia Commons, CC BY-SA 2.0; **24** *cla*: Jarvis Cocker © livepict.com, Wikimedia Commons, CC BY-SA 3.0; **24** *clb*: Wendell Pierce © Philip Romano, Wikimedia Commons, CC BY-SA 4.0; **25** *cla*: Brad Pitt © Glenn Francis, www.PacificProDigital.com, Wikimedia Commons, CC BY-SA 4.0; **25** *clb row 1*: James May © Khairil Zhafri, Wikimedia Commons, CC BY-SA 2.0; **25** *clb row 1*: George Monbiot © John Russell, Wikimedia Commons, CC BY-SA 2.0; **25** *crb row 1*: Vanessa Williams © Angela George, Wikimedia Commons, CC BY-SA 3.0; **25** *clb row 2*: Peter Jones © TheRangePress, Wikimedia Commons, CC BY-SA 3.0; **25** *cb row 2*: David Thewlis © Andreas Tai, Wikimedia Commons, CC BY-SA 3.0; **25** *crb row 2*: Mike Myers © Caroline Bonarde Ucci, Wikimedia Commons, CC BY-SA 3.0; **25** *clb row 3*: Jason Isaacs © DoD News Features, Wikimedia Commons, CC BY-SA 2.0; **25** *cb row 3*: Helen Hunt © Smokeonthewater, Wikimedia Commons, CC BY-SA 4.0; **25** *crb row 3*: Norman Cook © Shokophoto, Wikimedia Commons, CC BY-SA 2.0; **25** *clb row 4*: Lisa Kudrow © makoto2007, Wikimedia Commons, CC BY-SA 2.0; **25** *cb row 4*: Emmanuelle Béart © Georges Biard, Wikimedia Commons, CC BY-SA 3.0; **25** *crb row 4*: Sanjeev Bhaskar © TheAsianAwards, Wikimedia Commons, CC BY-SA 3.0; **25** *clb row 5*: Johnny Marr © University of Salford Press Office, Wikimedia Commons, CC BY-SA 2.0; **25** *cb row 5*: Ian Wright © James Boyes, Wikimedia Commons, CC BY-SA 2.0; **29** *bl*: C.S. Lewis © Aronsyne, Wikimedia Commons, CC BY-SA 4.0; **31** *tl*: Coins © Jo Smiley Hailey, Unsplash.com; **31** *tr*: House © Sludgegulper, Wikimedia Commons, CC BY-SA 2.0; **31** *cl*: Ford Cortina © Charles01, Wikimedia Commons, CC BY-SA 3.0; **31** *bl*: Typewriter © Rainer P. A. Wermke, Wikimedia Commons, CC BY-SA 4.0; **31** *bc*: Milk Bottles © Jason Murphy, Unsplash.com; **31** *br*: Petrol Station © Erik Mclean, Unsplash.com; **32** *tr*: Malaysian plantation kindly supplied by ex-Plantation Manager John Lewis; **34** *tc*: IR8 Seeds © IRRI (www.irri.org), Wikimedia Commons, CC BY-SA 3.0; **34** *tr*: Barrels © Bbadgett, Wikimedia Commons, CC BY-SA 3.0; **40** *cra*: Gratin Dauphinois © Ludovic Péron, Wikimedia Commons, CC BY-SA 3.0; **41** *c*: Spotted Dick © Tracy, Wikimedia Commons, CC BY-SA 2.0; **42** *cra*: SS Canberra © John Ward, Wikimedia Commons, CC BY-SA 4.0; **43** *all images*: © with thanks to Jenny Finch; **47** *tl*: Tom Courtenay © Allan warren, Wikimedia Commons, CC BY-SA 3.0; **50** *tl*: The Tardis © aussiegall, Wikimedia Commons, CC BY-SA 2.0; **51** *tl*: Des O'Connor © Archives New Zealand, Wikimedia Commons, CC BY-SA 2.0; **52** *bl*: Cathy McGowan © Paul Townsend, Wikimedia Commons, CC BY-SA 2.0; **53** *tr*: BBC Broadcasting House © Redvers, Wikimedia Commons, CC BY-SA 3.0; **57** *cla* & *clb*: Frank Ifield © Bradford Timeline, Flickr, CC BY-SA 2.0; **58** *tl*: Bob Dylan © Joe Gratz, Wikimedia Commons, CC BY-SA 2.0; **58** *bl*: Leeds Town Hall © Leeds Piano Competition 2015, Wikimedia Commons, CC BY-SA 2.0; **59** *br*: Nana Mouskouri © Ron Kroon for Anefo, Wikimedia Commons, CC BY-SA 3.0; **60** *cl*: Roy Lichtenstein © Eric Koch for Anefo, Wikimedia Commons, CC BY-SA 3.0; **60** *br*: Allan Kaprow © Dictioneer, Wikimedia Commons, CC BY-SA 4.0; **61** *tl* & **62** *cl* & **63** *tl* & **63** *bl*: original artwork created with the assistance of AI using Dall-E2 and Stable Diffusion; **61** *cl*: Hand with lights (m) © Diego PH, Unsplash.com; **61** *bl*: Butterflies (m) © Ksenia Makagonova, Unsplash.com; **61** *bl*: Key (m) © Everyday basics, Unsplash.com; **62** *tl*: Gorilla (m) © Joshua J. Cotten, Unsplash.com; **62** *tl*: Skiing (m) © Robinseed, Wikimedia Commons, CC BY-SA 4.0; **63** *cl*: Child reading (m) © Jonathan Borba, Unsplash.com; **65** *br*: Carol Ann Duffy © walnut whippet, Wikimedia Commons, CC BY-SA 2.0; **66** *bl*: Valentina Tereshkova © RIA Novosti archive, image #616304 / Alexander Mokletsov, Wikimedia Commons, CC BY-SA 3.0; **67** *bl*: Arecibo Observatory © H. Schweiker/WIYN and NOAO/AURA/NSF, Wikimedia Commons, CC BY-SA 4.0; **68** *cra*: Dr. Starzl operating in 1963 © with thanks to Dr. Thomas E. Starzl website, www.starzl.pitt.edu; **68** *tr*: SRI Computer Mouse © SRI International, Wikimedia Commons, CC BY-SA 3.0; **68** *crb*: Hypertext diagram © Andreariverac, Wikimedia Commons, CC BY-SA 3.0; **70** *tl*: Mellotron © Buzz Andersen, Wikimedia Commons, CC BY-SA 2.0; **71** *clb*: Audio Cassette © Thegreenj, Wikimedia Commons, CC BY-SA 3.0; **72** *cla*: Cliveden © Daderot, Wikimedia Commons, CC BY-SA 3.0; **73** *tr*: Bridego Bridge © Sealman, Wikimedia Commons, CC BY-SA 3.0; **74** *br*: Dr. Martin Luther King Jr. © National Park Service, Wikimedia Commons, CC BY-SA 2.0; **76** *cl*: Dr. Richard Beeching © urban_outlaw, Flickr.com, CC BY-SA 2.0; **76** *crb*: Prospect Tunnel © TJBlackwell, Flickr.com, CC BY-SA 3.0; **77** *tr*: East Dundry Lane © HowardDublin, Wikimedia Commons, CC BY-SA 4.0; **77** *cl*: Old Farm © Richard Johnson, Wikimedia Commons, CC BY-SA 2.0; **77** *br*: Ormerod House© Richard Johnson, Wikimedia Commons, CC BY-SA 2.0; **78** *tr*: Region 6 War Room© Chris Wood, Wikimedia Commons, CC BY-SA 4.0; **78** *crb*: Barnton Quarry Bunker © AlasdairW, Wikimedia Commons, CC BY-SA 3.0; *(continued on next page...)*

Photo Credits continued

81 *tr*: Chuck McKinley © Keystone Press / Alamy Stock Photo; **82** *br*: Swinton rugby club © Blue Monkey, Wikimedia Commons, CC BY-SA 3.0; **83** *t*: West Indies Cricket Team © PA Images / Alamy Stock Photo; **84** *tr*: Arkle and Mill House © PA Images / Alamy Stock Photo; **85** *bl*: Ford GT40 © Lothar Spurzem, Wikimedia Commons, CC BY-SA 2.0; **87** *tr*: Bob Charles © World Golf Hall of Fame, facebook.com/GolfHallofFame/; **87** *br*: Sewsunker Sewgolum © Harry Smith/Sportracepower, sportracepower.wordpress.com; **88** *t*: Aston Martin DB5 © DeFacto, Wikimedia Commons, CC BY-SA 4.0; **88** *b*: Mercedes 230 SL © Lothar Spurzem, Wikimedia Commons, CC BY-SA 2.0; **89** *b*: Lear Jet 23 © Michael Barera, Wikimedia Commons, CC BY-SA 4.0; **90** *t*: Lava Lamps © Dean Hochman, Wikimedia Commons, CC BY-SA 2.0; **90** *b*: Kodak Instamatic 50 © Friedrich Haag, Wikimedia Commons, CC BY-SA 4.0; **91** *b*: Tetra Pak Tetra Brik © Tetra Pak, Wikimedia Commons, CC BY-SA 2.0; **94** *tc*: Coffee Table (m) © Sincerely Media, Unsplash.com; **BC** *tl*: Martine Carol (m) © Boris Carmi /Meitar Collection / National Library of Israel / The Pritzker Family National Photography Collection, Wikimedia Commons, CC BY-SA 4.0; **BC** *tr*: Marlene Dietrich (m) © Eric Koch / Anefo, Wikimedia Commons, CC BY-SA 3.0; **BC** *tr*: Pele (m) © Gelderen, Hugo van / Anefo, Wikimedia Commons, CC BY-SA 3.0;

Graphic and Background Image Credits

Credits shown in the order in which they appear in the book.

Additional Key

(ic) = icon; (ph) = photo

fc *c*, **tp** *ca*, **bc** *w*: (ph) Texture by Felipe Santana, Unsplash; **cp, 3-17**: (ph) Wood by Michael Schwarzenberger, Pixabay; **2-3, 18-94** *tb*: (m)(ph) Paper Texture by rawpixel.com; **3** *cla*: (ic) Play by Adrien Coquet, thenounproject.com, CC BY-SA 3.0; **6,8,10,12,14,16** *tl* & **7,9,11,13,15,17** *tr*: (ic) Newspaper by Loic Poivet, thenounproject.com, CC BY-SA 3.0; **6-17** *c*: (ph) Book by Robert Armstrong, Pixabay; **18-29,46-65,88-94** *w*: (m)(ph) Concrete texture by rawpixel.com; **18,20,22,24** *tl* & **17,19,21,23,25** *tr*: (ic) Birthday Calendar by Kiran Shastry, thenounproject.com, CC BY-SA 3.0; **18** *cla*: (ic) Football by leo-graph.com, thenounproject.com, CC BY-SA 3.0; **18** *clb*: (ic) Basketball by Rabi'ah Al Adawiyyah, thenounproject.com, CC BY-SA 3.0; **19,22,24** *cla* & **23** *clb* & **29** *tl*: (ic) Music Note by Karen Tyler, thenounproject.com, CC BY-SA 3.0; **19,21,24** *clb* & **25** *cla*: (ic) Clapper Board by Andrew Nielsen, thenounproject.com, CC BY-SA 3.0; **20** *cla*: (ic) Television by Adrien Coquets, thenounproject.com, CC BY-SA 3.0; **20** *clb*: (ic) Chess by Hilmy Abiyyu Asad, thenounproject.com, CC BY-SA 3.0; **21,23** *cla*: (ic) Theatre Comedy by B Farias, thenounproject.com, CC BY-SA 3.0; **22** *clb*: (ic) Palette by ciciliakwo, thenounproject.com, CC BY-SA 3.0; **25** *clb*: (ic) Baby by Emily Keller, thenounproject.com, CC BY-SA 3.0; **26,28** *tl* & **27,29** *tr*: (ic) Wreath by Alex Muravev, thenounproject.com, CC BY-SA 3.0; **28** *tl*: (ic) Speaker by popcornarts, thenounproject.com, CC BY-SA 3.0; **28** *cl* & **28** *bl* : (ic) poet by Phạm Thanh Lộc, thenounproject.com, CC BY-SA 3.0; **29** *cl* & **29** *bl*: (ic) Book by Travis Avery, thenounproject.com, CC BY-SA 3.0; **30** *tl* & **31** *tr*: (ic) Coins by Evgenii Likhachov, thenounproject.com, CC BY-SA 3.0; **30-44** *w*: (m)(ph) White Concrete Wall by rawpixel.com; **32** *tl*: (ic) Earth by David Khai, thenounproject.com, CC BY-SA 3.0; **33** *tr*: (ic) Office by Anggara Putra, thenounproject.com, CC BY-SA 3.0; **34** *tl*: (ic) Tractor by Olivier Guin, thenounproject.com, CC BY-SA 3.0; **35** *tr*: (ic) School Desk by Jongrak, thenounproject.com, CC BY-SA 3.0; **36** *tl*: (ic) Exams by Arjan Farzkenari, thenounproject.com, CC BY-SA 3.0; **37** *tr*: (ic) Children by IronSV, thenounproject.com, CC BY-SA 3.0; **38** *tl* & **39** *tr*: (ic) Home by Numero Uno, thenounproject.com, CC BY-SA 3.0; **40** *tl*: (ic) Potato by Firza Alamsyah, thenounproject.com, CC BY-SA 3.0; **41** *tr*: (ic) Pudding by Ranah Pixel Studio, thenounproject.com, CC BY-SA 3.0; **42** *tl* & **43** *tr*: (ic) Holiday by Claudia Revalinap, thenounproject.com, CC BY-SA 3.0; **44** *tl*: (ic) Fashion by Mahmure Alp, thenounproject.com, CC BY-SA 3.0; **45** *tr*: (ic) Christmas Tree by Azam Ishaq, thenounproject.com, CC BY-SA 3.0; **41** *w*: Christmas (m) © Annie Spratt, Unsplash.com; **46** *tl*: (ic) Entertainment by shashank singh, thenounproject.com, CC BY-SA 3.0; **47,49** *tr* & **48** *tl*: (ic) Clapper Board by Andrew Nielsen, thenounproject.com, CC BY-SA 3.0; **50,52** *tl* & **51** *tr*: (ic) Old TV by Eko Purnomo, thenounproject.com, CC BY-SA 3.0; **53** *tr*: (ic) Radio by GreenHill, thenounproject.com, CC BY-SA 3.0; **54,56** *tl* & **55** *tr*: (ic) Record by Mourad Mokrane, thenounproject.com, CC BY-SA 3.0; **57** *tr*: (ic) Music Note by Karen Tyler, thenounproject.com, CC BY-SA 3.0; **58** *tl* & **59** *tr*: (ic) Trumpet by Valter Bispo, thenounproject.com, CC BY-SA 3.0; **60** *tl*: (ic) Arts by Kelsey Armstrong, thenounproject.com, CC BY-SA 3.0; **61,63** *tr* & **62** *tl*: (ic) Book by Travis Avery, thenounproject.com, CC BY-SA 3.0; **64** *tl*: (ic) Theatre by Ben Davis, thenounproject.com, CC BY-SA 3.0; **65** *tr*: (ic) Poetry by Martin, thenounproject.com, CC BY-SA 3.0; **66-71** *w*: (ph) Electricity (m) © Hal Gatewood, Unsplash.com; **66** *tl* & **67** *tr*: (ic) Saturn by Trevor Dsouza, thenounproject.com, CC BY-SA 3.0; **68** *tl*: (ic) Medicine Bottle by Muhammad Nur Auliady Pamungkas, thenounproject.com, CC BY-SA 3.0; **68** *tr*: (ic) Computer games by Symbolon, thenounproject.com, CC BY-SA 3.0; **70** *tl*: (ic) Piano by b farias, thenounproject.com, CC BY-SA 3.0; **71** *tr*: (ic) Speaker by Ryan Adryawan, thenounproject.com, CC BY-SA 3.0; **72** *tl*: (ic) unlike by Jems Mayor, thenounproject.com, CC BY-SA 3.0; **72** *w*: (ph) Houses of Parliament (m) © vwalakte, Freepik.com; **73** *tr* & **76** *tl*: (ic) Train by Sierra Pennala, thenounproject.com, CC BY-SA 3.0; **73** *w* & **76** *w*: (ph) Train Tracks (m) © Ben Garratt, Unsplash.com; **74** *tl* & **75** *tr*: (ic) Speaker by popcornarts, thenounproject.com, CC BY-SA 3.0; **74** *w*: (ph) Washington D.C. (m) © Mayer Tawfik, Unsplash.com; **75** *w*: (ph) Crowd (m) © davide ragusa, Unsplash.com; **77** *tr*: (ic) Snowflake by Adrien Coquet, thenounproject.com, CC BY-SA 3.0; **77** *w*: (ph) Snowscape (m) © Craig Whitehead, Unsplash.com; **78** *tl*: (ic) Ballistic Missile by Gabriel Baudon, thenounproject.com, CC BY-SA 3.0; **78** *w*: (ph) Radioactive gates (m) © Dan Meyers, Unsplash.com; **79** *tr*: (ic) spy by H Alberto Gongora, thenounproject.com, CC BY-SA 3.0; **79** *w*: (ph) Dark Tunnel (m) © Florian Pinkert, Unsplash.com; **80** *tl*: (ic) Football by leo-graph.com, thenounproject.com, CC BY-SA 3.0; **80** *w*: (ph) Football Pitch (m) © Alberto Frías, Unsplash.com; **81** *tr*: (ic) Tennis by Mister Pixel, thenounproject.com, CC BY-SA 3.0; **81** *w*: (ph) Tennis Court (m) © M. Z., Unsplash.com; **82** *tl*: (ic) Rugby Ball by Marco Livolsi, thenounproject.com, CC BY-SA 3.0; **82** *w*: (ph) Rugby Match (m) © Alex Motoc, Unsplash.com; **82** *h*: (ph) Rugby Lineout © Auckland Museum, Wikimedia Commons, CC BY-SA 4.0; **83** *tr*: (ic) Cricket by Bernd Lakenbrink, thenounproject.com, CC BY-SA 3.0; **83** *w*: (ph) Cricketer (m) © Yogendra Singh, Unsplash.com; **84** *tl*: (ic) Horse Racing by Sergio Morozov, thenounproject.com, CC BY-SA 3.0; **84** *w*: (ph) Racehorse (m) © Luisa Peter, Unsplash.com; **84** *h*: (ph) Horse Race © Jongsun Lee, Wikimedia Commons, CC BY-SA 3.0; **85** *tr*: (ic) Racing Car by Slidicon, thenounproject.com, CC BY-SA 3.0; **85** *w*: (ph) Chequered Flag (m) © Bas van den Eijkhof, Unsplash.com; **85** *h*: (ph) Race car (m) © Jeff Cooper, Unsplash.com; **86** *tl*: (ic) Boxing Glove by Anton Anuchin, thenounproject.com, CC BY-SA 3.0; **86** *w*: (ph) Boxing Match (m) © Johann Walter Bantz, Unsplash.com; **87** *tr*: (ic) Golfer by Nicolas Vicent, thenounproject.com, CC BY-SA 3.0; **87** *w*: (ph) Golfing (m) © Courtney Cook, Unsplash.com; **87** *h*: (ph) Golf Ball (m) © mk. s, Unsplash.com; **88,90** *tl* & **89,91** *tr*: (ic) Framed Picture by Lil Squid, thenounproject.com, CC BY-SA 3.0; **92** *tl* & **93** *tr*: (ic) Camera by AomAm, thenounproject.com, CC BY-SA 3.0; **94** *tl*: (ic) Present by Vinzence Studio, thenounproject.com, CC BY-SA 3.0

Join us for news on our future releases, reader promotions and behind-the-scenes content. All at:

www.subscribepage.com/whatayear

It's completely free to join. As a subscriber, we will email you no more than once or twice a month. We will never share your email address and you can unsubscribe at any time.

Answers to the Eleven-plus Exam on page 32

Arithmetic Questions

Q1: London to Birmingham is 120 miles
Q2: Christmas Day will fall on a Thursday
Q3: It will take 6 hours and 40 minutes
Q4: Five hundred and twenty three
Q5: A) John's mother was 40 years old
Q5: B) In 3 years' time
Q5: C) John will be 30 years old

General English Questions

Q1: A) Our dogs are carrying sticks.
Q1: B) Their butchers have no meat.
Q1: C) Men who like football are sure to have team scarves in their houses.
Q2: A) Finger
Q2: B) Umpire
Q2: C) Spaniards
Q3: A) Certain or sure
Q3: B) Shortly or soon
Q3: C) Decided

Printed in Great Britain
by Amazon

25148162R00053